# A LEADERSHIP CAROL
## A CLASSIC TALE FOR MODERN LEADERS

### JIM DITTMAR AND JOHN W. STANKO

# Table of Contents

# Foreword

I love this story. Funny thing, isn't it, that the coauthor of *The One Minute Manager*® would love a parable! I've found over the years that people learn best through stories—particularly ones they can identify with.

In *A Leadership Carol*, John and Jim begin with an all-too-familiar scenario that is known to bring down entire organizations: a self-serving leader who thinks all the brains are in his office. A leader who is profit-focused and ego-driven. A leader who hasn't yet realized that "none of us is as smart as all of us."

Most self-serving leaders who fail don't get a second chance. But when our central character, Ben, makes a decision that clashes with his leadership team's last ditch effort to save his failing organization, he is given an opportunity to see the problems created by his self-serving style. With the help of three consultants and his great-grandfather, Ben faces the facts—and discovers that the old way of doing things might be the best way, after all.

I recommend you get personally involved in the message of *A Leadership Carol* by occasionally asking the question "What can I learn from this journey?" as you are reading. If you do this, *A Leadership Carol* will speak to you in a way that could make a big difference for you and those you lead. But don't apply your learnings only in the workplace. Take them with you into your home and community—because effective leadership is effective leadership, no matter where it is practiced.

Thanks, John and Jim, for the great story and the positive effect it will have on your readers and the people in their lives.

Ken Blanchard, coauthor, *The New One Minute Manager® and One Minute Mentoring*

# Introduction

You hold in your hand a story that plays out regularly in business settings all across this country and probably around the world. It is a story of a leader and the impact of his interactions with followers as they work, plan, dream, strategize, succeed, and fail together. This story contains all the drama and emotion of human life—anger, joy, confusion, betrayal, friendship, sadness, victory, frailty, weakness, and pride.

As you read this story, you may recognize some of the scenes as eerily familiar to those you encounter on a daily basis. That is because, as one wisdom writer once penned, "There is nothing new under the sun." The story has different characters carrying out unique work, but is repeated again and again as people join together to pursue mutual organizational purposes.

This story is divided into four acts and a finale, all centering around the reaction of Ben, the CEO of Always Watching Security Systems (AWSS) and the story's protagonist, to a consultant's report of his poor performance as a leader. The four acts are followed by the report itself. In the consultants' report, you will read the authors' summary of what needs to take place for this story and for your story to have a happy ending. The last section of the book will contain some additional thoughts from the authors, in interview format, to help you understand even more of the tale you are about to read.

You may recognize a familiar story line as you read, and that is purely intentional. The circumstances have been adjusted to fit the modern world, but the human dynamics revealed in the following pages are as old as time itself. The authors present their version of this drama in the hopes that happier stories may emerge as leaders and their teams grapple with the issues of the day, and produce their own multi-act plays in which they are the stars and by which audiences can learn to appreciate the effort that goes into producing a successful business performance.

We trust that you will insert your own leadership style and your current leadership scenario that is playing out in your church, business, or institution into this fable as you read. You can ask yourself, "Is that indicative of my style? Is that how others perceive me? Perceive us? Is our team as together as we like to think that it is?" The consultant's report is purely fictional, but it is actually made up of real-life experiences that the authors have had as we acted out our roles in modern society.

We hope you enjoy *A Leadership Carol*, and we present it with the hope that it stimulates thought and discussion in your world of business concerning how we can join together to produce happier, healthier, and more productive interactions and business results that are the rule and not the exception.

Jim Dittmar
John W. Stanko
July 2017

# The story

# ACT ONE

Ben looked at his watch and thought, *It can't be just two minutes since I last looked! When's this session going to end? This is absurd!*

Ben was in a conference room with his management team, and they were participating in what was supposed to be a team-building session with a consultant he had been coerced to hire to put some fire under his underperforming team. This was the fourth of five days that the consultant was at the company, and Ben's patience, not something he was noted for in the first place, had just about expired.

Francis Johnson, the consultant, was using an old-fashioned overhead projector with transparencies to plot the personality styles of each team member. *Who still uses an overhead projector?* Ben thought to himself. Yet Ben was the only one who seemed to notice or mind that fact. What's more, the team seemed to be engrossed in Francis' presentation, much to Ben's amazement—and annoyance.

"You see here," Francis explained. "Cheryl's the most relational of the team. She never met a stranger and loves to talk to everyone." Francis paused to allow the laughter to subside as the rest of the team looked at one another and nodded in agreement.

*This is so ridiculous*, Ben thought, as Francis continued to analyze Cheryl, the office manager. Also in the room were Jimmy, Ben's nephew, who was the vice-president for business development; Jeff Collins, the CFO; Abdul Mohammed, the CIO; and Charlene Harkins, the COO.

"And then there's Jeff," Francis continued. "Don't approach Jeff without an appointment two days in advance. Cheryl never met a detail she liked, and Jeff never met one that wasn't his friend." Again, the team affirmed what Francis was saying through laughter and shouts of, "That's so true!" Ben did not participate in the frivolity. *We're going down the tubes, and this is how we spend our time?* Ben thought to himself.

"That's why Jeff and Cheryl make a great team, because they're so different and can complement one another in the work they do," Francis explained. He paused to replace the transparency on the projector, "And Charlene's the perfect fit for Jeff and Cheryl because she's both organized and relational. She can work with either, and round out the office team." Charlene was obviously pleased and took it all in, taking notes as Francis spoke.

Ben, who was CEO of his family's fourth-generation security firm, was not pleased. He sat at the head of the table and did a slow boil. Ben was perturbed that people were buying into this concept, and he didn't like it one bit. Then Francis crossed the line.

"Let's look at Ben," Francis continued, and the room fell eerily quiet. "Ben's the boss in all things. He believes his ideas are better than everyone else's ideas combined!" The team shot nervous glances toward Ben, who had a cold, fake half-smile on his face as he stared straight at Francis, never looking at anyone else.

"It's pretty much impossible for Ben to say he's sorry, for he seldom is," Francis continued. "Ben believes that would make him look weak, and his style doesn't ever want to look weak." Ben chimed in, "Yep, that's pretty much like me," but his intent was not to agree, but rather to bring the session to an end.

What's more, Ben didn't simply intend to end this session. He had every intention of ending Francis' work with Ben's company the first chance he had. It didn't matter that the people seemed to relate to what was going on, Ben thought it was a lot of psycho-babble, and it was about to come to end before tomorrow's planned wrap up meeting.

"Jeff, have you cut Francis' check for services rendered yet?" Ben asked his CFO as the participants filed out of the conference room.

"Why, no, I had not. I thought I would mail it to him as I always do," Jeff responded.

"Let's write it now before the end of the year and give it to Francis to take home with him," Ben suggested. "Give it to me today so I can have it for tomorrow." Jeff thought the request a bit unusual, but he complied, dropping off the check before he left for the evening.

Ben's company was Always Watching Security Systems (AWSS). It had been founded by Ben's great-grandfather, who had come to the United States from England right before the turn of the century. Eventually, his great-grandfather had started a security company at a time when America needed protection for its expanding banking, railroad, and corporate sectors.

AWSS started small, but found its niche in New Jersey where Ben's family lived, focusing on providing security for banks and other financial institutions. Eventually, the company provided services for many of the seaports in northern New Jersey.

The company had weathered several depressions, the proliferation of other security companies, two world wars, and numerous cultural and technological changes to become a multi-million-dollar entity. Their distinctive green uniforms with the corporate logo—an eye within the map of the U.S.—had strong brand recognition, especially on the East Coast.

Ben's great-grandfather's name was Fred Holiday. He had settled in the northern Jersey area after emigrating from England. The only job he could find at first was as a warehouse night security guard. He saw an opportunity to start something of his own to care for his wife and three sons, so he founded AWSS in 1902. One of those three sons was Ben's grandfather, also named Ben Holiday, who when it was his turn, went into the business, climbing to the top of the company through his ability to find new clients and sources for AWSS guards. Great-grandfather Fred had a good understanding of branding, even back in the early 1900s, and was the one who introduced the green uniforms at a time when everything in the world of uniforms seemed to be either black or navy blue.

The company benefitted from the outbreak of World War I, partnering with the Department of Defense to provide security at the New Jersey ports, which saw increased ship traffic as more and more war equipment and troops were sent off to the European front. AWSS used its extensive New Jersey contacts and clients to be the eyes and ears for the U.S. Government, actually getting involved in some spying activities on Americans of German descent. This aspect of the business would prove to be lucrative, but in time would cause the problems with which Ben was grappling at the moment.

After World War I, boom times came in the U.S., and AWSS was in on the action. America's manufacturing prowess continued to expand, which led to more and more exports, and more and more companies that needed reliable security services to protect themselves from thievery and, at times, from their own employees, who filed false injury claims and pilfered company property and goods. That is when AWSS branched out to provide private investigation services, and they became known as the company, like the Canadian Mounties, who "always got their man" (or woman). Speaking of Canada, AWSS did some work in Ontario for the U.S. Government, which was the start of their international service division.

The boom times ended, as they always do, and the U.S. growth of the '20s ended in the Great Depression of the '30s. AWSS saws its business plummet as some of their clients went out of business since the New York and New Jersey areas were hit hardest. Some companies brought their security in-house and others had nothing to secure—they were bankrupt. AWSS fell back on its core business upon which it was founded—private security guards—and they slashed prices and costs to stay alive. Great-grandfather Fred brought the entire family into the business where his sons served as guards and his daughters worked in the office. Somehow, the company made it through, and the boom times returned when Word War II approached.

At that time, the Federal Government needed AWSS' services again, and by the late '30s into the '40s, Defense Department money helped turn the tide in AWSS' favor, and the company was able to expand and thrive once again. As espionage and the business of war became more sophisticated, so did AWSS. Grandfather

Ben brought his youthful zeal and ideas to the company, and they began to branch out beyond the traditional security guard core into things like installing security alarm systems and conducting background checks for companies that needed high security screening services. There were rumors that AWSS had also cooperated in what would become illegal wire-tapping services for the government, but there was never any proof or charges filed. Eventually, AWSS got into drug testing and background checks for more routine hires.

Grandfather Ben Holiday and his wife had four children, three girls and one boy. The boy, Albert Holiday, was third in the birth order. Born in 1942, Ben's father, Albert, at first had little interest in AWSS. He loved sports and had an artistic side that his father, Ben's grandfather, did not understand—or appreciate. Albert wanted to be an artist and pursued art in school, even into university. Albert did not do well in school, however, and dropped out in 1960. At that point, he had no choice but to go into the family business. At first, Albert gravitated toward marketing where he could at least design some advertising campaigns, but eventually got pulled into other parts of the business that involved computers, since everyone else was frightened by the thought of the computer age.

Ben's father got into computers, even though they were not widely used except for some government defense work and in university research. Albert saw their possible use in security work and their potential for the company. Albert spent more and more time in Washington, D.C. courting government military officials, learning what he could about the future, and understanding sophisticated surveillance equipment and practices. Eventually, this would become the core of the company, but still they employed security guards who wore the company green uniforms. In fact, green was the company color, even as it went increasingly digital.

Albert married Louise in 1964 and they had three children: Ben was the oldest and was named after his Grandfather Ben. Then his sister Miriam was born, and finally his little brother, Thomas. Ben was born in 1967 and his other two siblings were born two years apart in 1969 and 1971. His family lived in Englewood, New Jersey, and his father could almost walk to the AWSS offices that were also located in Englewood. Ben was not that interested in the company when he was growing up—just like his father—but eventually he became intrigued with the possibilities of him being the fourth generation of Holidays to work for and lead the company.

In 1988, after graduating from Dartmouth with a degree in accounting and business management, Ben came right into the company as director of business development. His sister also went to an Ivy League school, attending Princeton, where she majored in business with a focus on marketing and public relations. She went on to get her MBA and, after working for McKinsey and Company, she founded her own consulting firm. In fact, Francis, who was doing the team building at AWSS, came from Miriam's company.

Unfortunately, Ben's sister Miriam had died at a young age of breast cancer, and two of her children continued their mother's consulting business. Miriam's third child, Jimmy, was part of the AWSS team, representing yet another generation of Holidays at AWSS. Ben, who had never married, was not as impressed as he once was with the family tradition of hiring family, and was more interested in running a successful business.

He was an accountant and the numbers didn't lie. The truth was that AWSS was in some trouble. The fact that Francis came from his sister's company made what

Ben was going to do in the morning all the more difficult, but he didn't care. He wasn't going to surrender control of his company or his management style to someone telling him he needed to understand his people in order to build a better team. He knew what he needed to do to improve his team, and that was going to start before the planned debriefing meeting with Francis the next morning at 10 AM.

As Ben made his way to his Manhattan office the next morning, he used the train ride from his home in Stamford, Connecticut to outline in his mind what he was going to say to Francis. When he arrived, Francis was already in the office conference room, setting up some props for his presentation, which included the projector and some things he had already written on the white board.

"Good morning, Mr. Holiday," Francis said as Ben entered the room.

"Hello, Francis," responded Ben. "You're here bright and early."

"Yes sir. We have a lot of ground to cover today," Francis responded enthusiastically.

"Uh, yes, Francis, I'd like to talk to you in my office about the day's proceedings," Ben said in a cold, foreboding tone. "May I see you there now?"

Francis was fairly young and inexperienced, so he didn't read the signs present in Ben's voice, body language, or demeanor. Like a lamb being led to the slaughter, Francis followed Ben into his corner office. It was the same office where Francis had interviewed Ben as part of his week-long visit to get to the bottom of what was wrong at AWSS.

Francis suddenly had a flashback of how difficult that interview had been. He had included that fact in his report, which he had stayed up to finish until 1:45 AM. He was tired but excited about what he had found. He was confident he was on the right track to help get AWSS out of its rut and back in the black.

Francis naively and nervously blurted out, "I'm excited about today, Mr. Holiday. I think you'll be pleased with the results. I also think AWSS has some difficult issues to face, but I don't see why they can't be addressed."

Ben responded, "Well, Francis, I'm not pleased with the results and I haven't even seen the results. I decided during yesterday's team meeting that I had to do something that you're probably not going to like very much."

"What's that?" asked Francis.

"I've decided that AWSS no longer needs the services of you or your company," Ben said coldly, watching Francis closely for his reaction.

Francis sat in stunned silence, his face showing the shock from the words he had just heard. Ben was enjoying what he saw, mostly because he had the upper hand.

"When you came in, it was at the suggestion of my nephew, Jimmy, who really insisted that the problem here was our culture that lacked trust, exercised poor communication, and employed sloppy hiring practices," Ben explained.

"I wasn't that excited about it, but I thought, 'Hey, my father gave me a chance to make a difference in AWSS, so I needed to do that for Jimmy,'" Ben continued. "I also thought I could help my sister's firm as I kept my nephew happy. But when you started in with all that personality stuff yesterday, I made up my mind. There's no need for you to continue today."

Francis was by then flushed and could feel himself

begin to perspire under his dress shirt. "But Mr. Holiday, I have this report for you and your team, and I really think it's going to help you . . ."

Ben interrupted him before Francis could finish. "I don't need that report, Francis. You're going to tell me about my people and how I need to build a better team. You'll tell me I need to communicate more effectively and listen more intently," Ben said, trying to show Francis that he already understood some of the principles that Francis was going to share.

"The truth is, Francis, I don't need someone to tell me about my people. I know they're basically lazy and I need someone to help me get them straight, not explain whether or not they're into details or change," Ben said, stopping to let that settle into Francis' thinking.

"I need people who won't surrender when the press gets a little hostile. I need people who will stay the course—the course that I set for the company. I need people who will do what I say, for after all, I'm the CEO. They have to adjust to me, not me to them."

Francis was frantically searching his mind for something to say, something that would convince Mr. Holiday that he was mistaken, that Francis could help. "Sir, if you would just give this a chance. I realize you know about some of these leadership practices, and applying them will require some new ways of doing things, but I . . ."

Again, Ben cut him off. "I'm not interested in your report, Francis. In fact, I won't even accept or look at it! I have your check ready to go, and please bill us for any expenses that we have not covered so far. Other than that, Francis, I think we are through here." Ben handed Francis the envelope with the check.

It was 8:30 and Francis had thought the meeting would start at 10:00. As it turned out, he would not even be in the office by then. There were no handshakes or pleasantries exchanged, and Francis stood for a few seconds, still hoping to find something that could salvage his week's work at AWSS. Ben stood behind his desk, at that point checking his smartphone for messages and looking for the daily report he received every morning of the night's activities.

Francis got up and noticed that his shirt was wet with perspiration, stuck to his back through his undershirt. He hoped Ben would not notice. Francis returned to the conference room and packed up the things he had brought. He put them all in his wheeled briefcase and started for the elevator. As he did, he passed Ben's nephew Jimmy's, who was in his office, checking his emails.

"Hey there, Francis, this is the big day! Where are you going? Forget something?" Jimmy inquired.

"No, it isn't the big day, Jimmy," Francis said, his voice quivering.

"What do you mean?" Jimmy asked with a furrow in his brow.

"Uh, your Uncle Ben just dismissed me," Francis responded as he looked down at the floor. "He said he isn't interested in the report and had no further need for me or our services."

"That's crazy," Jimmy said with raised voice, "he can't be serious."

"Oh, I think he is, Jimmy, or I would not have packed up all my things," Francis said, his voice still a bit shaky.

Jimmy tried to make some sense of what Francis was saying. "Did he at least *look* at the report? Did you talk about any of the issues?"

"No sir. He said he didn't need a report that talked about team building or about a change to his leadership style. He needed help dealing with the lazy people he had on staff, people who would not stay the course when things got tough," Francis reported, still looking down, trying to control his emotions.

"Give me the report," Jimmy responded. "We're in trouble, and my uncle is going to face reality one way or the other!"

Francis began to recover his breath and composure, and said, "I'm sure you will be okay, Jimmy. After all, a $100-million-dollar company has the resources to recover. And AWSS' history goes back so far, you'll make it through somehow!" Francis was trying his best to put a positive spin on the negative situation.

"$100 million? Who told you that?" Jimmy snapped.

"Why, your uncle did?" Francis responded.

"That's a lie and part of the problem. He's in denial. He's an accountant, and he knows better. We were $100 million once but I promise you we aren't there now," Jimmy said with disgust. "Let me have it," Jimmy said.

"Excuse me?" Francis didn't quite hear understand what Jimmy was asking.

"Give *me* the report. If Uncle Ben won't receive the report from you, then he's going to get it from me, and he's going to read it or else!" Jimmy said, by that time trying to control his voice and emotions.

Francis opened his briefcase and handed Jimmy the report he had prepared. Jimmy held it and said, "Francis, you represented hope to all of us here, for you were the first one who spoke some truth to Uncle Ben, the first one to do so in a long time. I'm sorry this happened, but it probably needed to happen. You may have already helped us more than you know, but I'm so very sorry. Are you all right? Can I get you a taxi?"

"No, I'll be fine. I hope to catch an earlier flight

back home. If I can't, New York at Christmas time isn't a bad place to be stuck for a day," Francis said, trying to make the best of his redesigned day.

"Okay, well, thank you again. I'm so sorry for this trouble. When you see my family back in Indiana, tell them I said hello. A Merry Christmas to you and yours. And now it's time I go talk to my uncle and enter the arena of truth with him."

Before Francis was on the street and in a taxi, Jimmy was in Ben's office. "I know why you're here and nothing you can say is going to change my mind," Ben began before Jimmy could. "It was a waste of time."

"Waste of time?" Jimmy repeated. "You didn't even give it a chance or give *him* a chance. You pouted and sulked all week and had your mind made up."

"I wasn't pouting," Ben retorted. "I was sad that we had spent money at a time like this on something so frivolous, so trendy, so, so *stupid!*"

"And what's the idea of telling that guy our company had $100 million in annual revenue?" Jimmy continued with his offensive. "That was our peak four years ago. We haven't been close to that since."

Ben snapped back, "He had no business knowing our business. What's more, he would only go back to your mother's company and tell your siblings our business, which is no longer the family's business."

"Besides," Ben continued, "that had no relevance to the issue at hand, which was supposed to be getting you and the rest of your team off the Internet and into the things that are going to save this company."

"You are stubborn and it's going to ruin this company," Jimmy countered. "You broke your word because you promised to see this through with the consultant. What's more, the decisions you made, things that are all over the papers and television, are going to be our downfall. You just won't listen," Jimmy said disgustedly.

"See it through? To what? To hear that I need to be more engaging with my team? That I need to listen more? That I need to understand you better?" Ben asked in rapid-fire succession. "Yes, there needs to be some changes around here, but it's not me who needs to change."

Jimmy shot back, "We're all hanging on by a thread. After Tommy Morris quit because of your espionage program, we've lost a lot of other good folks and clients. Lately, it's been one bad event after another. Morale's already low."

Ben responded, "Morale is not my concern. The bottom line is my concern. We are paying these people to perform and be professionals. What Tommy did is done. I never did like him anyway. I agreed to bring Francis in to try and help us get back on track, at your recommendation, but yesterday's meeting was more than I'm ready to endure."

"Jeff, Cheryl, Abdul, Sharlene, and the others are all going to be devastated when they hear about this," Jimmy said shaking his head in disbelief. "I won't tell them anything now. It's almost Christmas and we have our holiday lunch this afternoon before the weekend. With Christmas next Tuesday, I have no intention of ruining their holiday with this news."

"I don't care what you tell them," Ben responded as he looked around his desk for something to do, signaling the conversation had come to an end, or at least that he was no longer interested in anything Jimmy had to say. Jimmy wasn't done, however, and in an uncharacteristic animated manner, he took the report and threw it down on his uncle's desk.

"There, if you're looking for something to do,

instead of looking for illegal work behind our backs, you can read the man's report and see what he had to say," Jimmy said, surprising even himself with his aggressive tone and action. "You either do that, or I'm out of here, family or no family," Jimmy yelled, again surprising himself with the force of his words.

"Fine," Ben said in a detached tone, "then maybe it's time to part ways."

"You can't be serious?" Jimmy shot back.

"I am," Ben said, using his coldest stare and with the iciest tone he could muster.

"I'm not going to accept that today," Jimmy said. "I'll give you the weekend to read this report. I'll tell the staff that Francis got called back home on pressing business and left the report for us to read and process during the holidays. You *will* read this or I *will* be gone. Think it over, Ben Holiday, the ball's in your court, and let's see what you do with it," Jimmy concluded.

"The ball has always been in my court, and it's my court and my ball," Ben answered. "And your role on the team, my dear nephew, may be coming to an end!"

The Christmas luncheon was held in the office to save some money. A Manhattan caterer brought in the usual fare—deli meat for sandwiches, all kinds of relishes, potato salad, soft drinks, chips, salsa, a veggie tray, and the like. The atmosphere was tense, and no one was in the holiday spirit.

"What do you think happened to Francis?" Abdul asked Cheryl. "Do you think he really got called back home?"

"I don't know what happened, but by the looks on Jimmy's and Ben's faces, I would say that the consultant had some things to say that didn't go over too well," Cheryl said in a hushed whisper so no one else would hear. Just then, Jeff came over with a plate of food and sat down.

"What are you guys talking about? Francis' vanishing act?" Jeff inquired.

"Yea, it's pretty strange. Do you know anything?" Abdul asked to neither of them in particular.

"I heard Ben and Jimmy in a serious, heated discussion when I came in this morning," Jeff responded. "Next thing I knew, Jimmy came out and said that Francis could not do the debrief today, but would be back, probably after the holidays, to finish it up. Ben had come in yesterday and wanted to make sure he had Francis' check, which I thought was strange, but that's the last I heard from anyone."

Cheryl chimed in, "I hope Francis will be back. We're still recovering from the debacle with Tommy. After he left, I lost hope. He was kind of the voice of reason, but was made to be the fall guy over the surveillance scandal. When it looked like we were going to address some of our demons, I was encouraged for the first time in years. Now, I'm not so sure . . ." Cheryl let her words trail off without finishing her thought.

Ben had no appetite for food or a party, so he fixed a plate, took it into his office, and closed the door to eat. Jimmy was there in body but did not engage in much conversation. When repeatedly asked about Francis, he simply said he had a family emergency and had to return to Indiana.

"My guess is that things didn't go well, that Ben didn't like what Francis was doing." Abdul chimed in. "Did you get a look at his face, especially in yesterday's session? He wasn't a happy camper!"

"Well, we're not happy campers either," said Cheryl. "It's hard to enjoy the holidays when you may not have a job after the first of the year, or when someone may be in jail!" Everyone nodded, and continued to consume their holiday fare as if it was their last meal.

⁑⁑⁑⁑⁑⁑⁑⁑⁑⁑ ⁑⁑ ⁑⁑

Ben could see everyone eating from his office window, which stretched from ceiling to floor. He had blinds that he kept at half mast, which enabled him to look out but prevented others from seeing in. That's the way he liked it. It galled him that the company was in such bad shape, and everyone was taking holiday time off and using up vacation before the year's end. There was work to do, reports to run, calls to make, and business to pursue.

Yet what could he or anyone do at this time of year. There was no new business to locate, no new strategies to unfold. Things were dead in the water, and if things didn't turn around quickly, AWSS would be finished. How did the business arrive at this crisis? What could he have done differently? He didn't start the practice of espionage and private investigation work. He just took it to the next level, but now all hell was breaking loose, and AWSS' clients were jumping ship at an alarming rate.

All he knew was that he couldn't stomach the office any longer, not as long as his ingrate nephew and his co-workers were conspiring against him, right outside his door! He was done for the day, so he gathered up his papers and decided he would get a jump on the weekend and avoid holiday rush hour. He headed over to Grand Central Station for an early train ride home to Stamford. Maybe there he could clear his head and breathe.

As he gathered up his papers to go home, Ben decided to put Francis' report in his briefcase. He flipped through it and saw it was 35-pages long, complete with charts and reports, but mostly narrative. Ben didn't want anyone to see or notice, but he would at least glance through the report in the privacy of his own home, away from the office that had become his personal chamber of horrors over the last two years.

# Act Two

The train ride to Stamford was less crowded than usual, since Ben had left New York so much earlier than he normally did. He didn't bother to say good-bye when he left, and he knew he would not see some of the staff on Monday because many had already started their holiday vacation a few days before Christmas. He noticed that his nephew Jimmy was in the office when he left. *Jimmy must have seen me leaving,* Ben thought, *but probably didn't realize I was going home. That's okay,* Ben reasoned, *for he won't be seeing much of me when he's left the company.*

Ben arrived at the Stamford station and walked to his car in the Park 'n Ride lot for the 10-minute drive home. The streets and stores were all decorated for the holidays, but Ben didn't much care. *There is too much emphasis on Christmas,* he thought, and he planned on working through the holiday as was his custom.

Ben walked through his front door at about 4 PM, and changed into his sweat pants and Green Bay Packers sweatshirt. He had been a Packers' fan since he was young for no good reason, and was looking forward to watching the Packers-Bears football game on Sunday night football. Other than that, he had no other plans for the weekend.

As Ben got comfortable, his thoughts turned to dinner, since he had consumed very little of the party food at the office. He opened the freezer and found a lasagna meal that he popped into the microwave and also pulled a ready-made salad from his refrigerator along with a Heineken. He ate and drank while he watched the news on TV. As he watched, the business news came on.

He watched with discomfort as the cable channel ran a story about AWSS and the controversial cell phone eavesdropping practice that had made the news over the last two years. People were shocked to find the government was in the business of spying on their own citizens, and the scandal and controversy would not go away. When the public found out that AWSS had colluded with the government to collect the information, people were concerned that AWSS was using their guards and security systems to do the same in their companies. That caused the mass client exodus that had the company in such poor financial shape.

Ben knew his company was being scrutinized, but he wasn't ready for more of this. His stock on the NASDAQ had opened years ago at $9 per share, quickly increased to $13, but then faded over the last two years until it was worth less than a dollar, which is when they pulled the stock from being listed. He thought by now the controversy would be over, but it was not. Ben had made the decision to enter the cell phone spy business and had not told anyone of his decision, except for the technicians who were needed to provide the technology to the Federal Government.

For a while, Ben had been wealthy, at least on paper, but he lost most of his wealth as the stock value evaporated. The thought of that made him angry, and now on top of that, his little snip of a nephew was giving him, the CEO, an ultimatum, "Read the report or I'll quit!" *Who does he think he is?* The more Ben thought about it, the angrier he got, and the more Heinekens he drank. Before he knew it, there were seven green bottles assembled on his living room coffee table. That being the case, Ben laid back on the couch, and before he knew it, he had dozed off.

He had been asleep for some time when the doorbell rang. *Now who could that be at this time on a Friday night?* Ben looked at his watch and it was 10:31 PM, and the TV was still on the news channel he had been watching. He decided to ignore the doorbell, but whoever it was kept ringing and ringing, and he finally decided that if he was going to get any more sleep, he had to answer it.

Ben went to the door, and yelled, "Who is it?" but there was no response. After repeating the question a few more times, the voice of an elderly man with a British accent answered back, "I have come to help you, Ben. I have come to save you and your company."

"What are you talking about? Who are you? Is this a joke?" Ben peeked out the peephole and saw an elderly gentleman dressed in what seemed to be rather old-fashioned but formal clothes.

"No, it's no joke and it's no joke the condition my company is in right now," the old man responded. "Now open the door! We need to talk."

"Old man, what do you mean *we* need to talk? And what do you mean *your* company?" This company has been in my family for four generations and I run it," Ben shouted through the door.

"That's right, Ben, you run it but I started it. This

is your Great-Grandfather Fred Holiday and we most certainly need to talk. Now let me in!"

. . . . . . . . . . .

Ben couldn't believe what he had just heard. He asked the man to repeat what he said. "Let me in, it's cold out here. I'm your great-grandfather," the voice impatiently shot back.

At that, Ben could not resist and opened the door. The man pushed against the door and walked into Ben's condo, looking around like it was his first time there, which of course it was.

"Nice place," the old man said. "Too bad you are about to lose it along with your company."

"I'm not losing anything," Ben said firmly. "And how do you know so much about me and my company?"

"I told you, I'm your great-grandfather, Fred Holiday. I started AWSS in 1902, and I didn't start it for someone like you to come along and ruin it. Now we have some work to do and only a little time to do it. Where can we talk?" the old man said, seizing control of the meeting.

As he said that, Ben's great-grandfather took off his overcoat, which revealed that he was in formal eveningwear for the occasion. He made his way into the living room where Ben had been asleep, and picked up one of the beer bottles.

"Heineken? A German beer? Where I came from in England, we would *never* drink German beer," the old man complained. It was then that Ben again detected an English accent as the old man spoke. *Whoever he is, he's a good actor*, Ben thought, but Ben knew his family had their ancestral roots in England.

"All right, tell me what you came here to tell me that's so urgent," Ben said sarcastically.

"That's your problem, Ben," the old man

responded. "You don't think anyone has anything to tell you. You know *everything*."

"You don't know me," Ben sneered, "and even if you did, your day has passed. You would have nothing to say about business that would interest me."

At that point, the man raised his walking stick as if he were going hit Ben over the head with it. "Know nothing? You idiot? I've forgotten more about business than you ever knew," the old man snorted. "My spirit has watched over the company these many decades, living through the vision and mission that I established and my son, your grandfather, continued," the old man said angrily, but when he mentioned his son, his face and tone softened.

"We brought this company through wars and depressions, and now you've just about ransacked it with your arrogance and rudeness," the man said as he stared at Ben, shaking his head in pity and disgust.

Ben was thinking, *Is this real? I must be dreaming!* Ben had to admit that this guy, whoever he was, did look like the picture of the company's founder that formerly hung in the board room at work, before it was replaced by a big screen TV.

"Pay attention, Ben, for my carriage is waiting outside and will be leaving momentarily. Your nephew handed you a report. Where is it?" Ben was startled, for how could the old man have known about the report?

"Yea, I brought it home," Ben said as he went for his briefcase to retrieve the report. When he found it, he held it up.

"That's it," the old man said. "What are you going to do with it?"

"Not much," Ben said, "Do you want to read it?" he said sarcastically.

The old man raised his stick one more time,

but decided against using it. "You're a smart aleck, and there's so little time. I'm not sure you can change," the man said sadly. "But we have no choice and must act quickly if we're going to save the company."

"Since you refuse to read the report or to hear what Francis has to say," the old man explained, "I'll have to bring the report to you. Francis was going to recommend that a team of consultants come to work with you to try and make you a better leader."

"Since you refused to see them at the office, they will come here. Throughout this weekend, three different consultants will come to visit you on three separate occasions. One will be the Spirit of Leadership Past, one the Spirit of Leadership Present, and the third the Spirit of Leadership Future." Ben was thinking, *I must have had some bad beer or the lasagna was tainted. This is too bizarre!*

Ben smiled wryly as if he were playing along with a joke. "Pay attention," the old man snapped. "That's another one of your problems among many. You don't listen very well."

"Do you understand your assignment?" the visitor asked. "Those three consultants will work with you to try and talk some sense into you. And then you *will* read the report. Is that clear? I have to go now, my carriage is waiting"

"Yes," said Ben, "unless I wake up first, old man."

"Don't call me, old man," the visitor snapped. "I'm your great-grandfather, but I can see you don't care. Instead of asking me questions about how to save the company, you're more interested in smarting off." At that, the old man proceeded back to the door. "Three consultants are coming to make sure you read that report! And one more thing. I would appreciate if you would put my picture back in the conference room where it belongs!"

26

With that, the elderly visitor put his coat back on and was gone, and Ben wasn't even sure he opened the door to exit.

*Whoa, no more falling asleep on the couch,* Ben thought, as he shook his head and looked out the peep hole, seeing nothing of a carriage or his strange visitor.

Ben woke up with a jump, as if someone shook him, but there was no one there.

*That was one strange dream, but it was so vivid,* he thought as he lay there on the couch, trying to get his bearings. It was 11:47 PM, and he wasn't sure how long he had been asleep. The TV was still on, and he went to his front door, opened it, and looked around, searching for what he did not know. There was no one and nothing out of the ordinary. Then Ben had to make a decision: Go right to bed, or stay up a few hours as the effects of his night nap kept him awake.

Ben decided for sleep, but on his way up the stairs to the bedroom, he went to his briefcase and pulled out the report that his dream visitor had admonished him to read. *If I can't sleep, then this will certainly put me out,* Ben thought, and had to chuckle at his own joke. There had not been many reasons to laugh lately.

As Ben crawled into bed, he turned on the light and stared at the front page of the report: A REPORT SUBMITTED TO MR. BEN HOLIDAY AT ALWAYS WATCHING SECURITY SERVICES: THE NEED FOR L.E.A.D.E.R.S. He opened to the next page and saw his company's logo with a brief summary of the company that produced the report: MCC Associates, and the MCC stood for Miriam's Consultants and Coaches.

Miriam was Ben's sister who had founded MCC in 2002. She had passed away in 2009 from breast cancer at the age of 43. The company was known for its emphasis on teamwork and leadership, and had creat-ed a consulting niche that had allowed the company to thrive, even after Miriam's death. Jimmy, Ben's nephew who issued the ultimatum, was Miriam's son, and it was his idea to bring in Miriam's firm to try to salvage AWSS.

*It was a bad idea to bring them in, Ben thought. They don't know the world of security; they don't under-stand Wall Street; and they certainly don't understand me and what I'm up against.*

Ben turned another page, which brought him to the Introduction:

> *In this report, we will evaluate the leadership at Always Watching Security Systems (AWSS) and specifically, Mr. Ben Holiday. This introduction will serve to explain what each of the letters in L.E.A.D.E.R.S. represents, with three key as-pects of each characteristic. We will then eval-uate AWSS in each area on a scale of Excellent, Good, Fair, and Poor. Following this introduction in our Consultant's Report, we provide further explanation of each leadership trait, and we provide an expanded description of what we found among AWSS' leadership and some steps the company can take, in partnership with our consultants, to enhance every area of the L.E.A.D.E.R.S. Model.*

Ben went on to the next page, realizing he was at the point where if he kept reading, he was going to be up for a while. He decided to take a peek at Section One. It began:

> *<u>Effective leaders foster influential relation-ships among followers</u>. Why? Because they real-ize that effective leadership is not just about "the leader," but understand that it's about engaging*

*in a process of leadership with followers, other leaders, customers, and other stakeholders. The ultimate objective of relational leadership is positive change and transformation for both their organizations and the people with whom they work.*

*This type of relational, transformative leadership process is inclusive by nature. For an organization to function at its best, leaders must embrace and take advantage of the diversity of perspectives, attitudes, skills, and insights represented within an organization.*

*AWSS Leadership Rating: POOR*

When Ben read that, he took the report and flung it across the room where it hit the wall and fell to the floor. "What do they mean a poor rating?" Ben yelled aloud. "He's young and a fool, and I'm glad I tossed his behind out on to the street! That report isn't worth the paper it's written on." With that, Ben rolled over and tried to sleep, hoping he had not passed the point of no return that would keep him up until 2 or later.

⁂

Ben did fall right to sleep but was awakened at some point during the night and noticed the lights were on in his den with the TV playing. *That's strange*, he thought, *I know I turned out the lights and turned off the TV.* Then he had the thought, *Maybe my great-grandfather is back, watching the business channel to see what he can learn!* Ben hated to get out of bed, and looked at the clock, which told him it was 1:41 AM.

As he went downstairs, Ben was shocked to see someone he didn't know sitting on his couch, with the remote control in his hand, watching TV. Ben screamed, "Hey, who the hell are you? And what are you doing here?"

The man was dressed casually and seated on the couch, eating popcorn and drinking one of Ben's Heinekens, didn't even look up from the TV when he answered, "Hey there, Ben, just waiting for you to get up and I thought I would watch some TV. By the way, I just saw the piece about AWSS. Tsk, tsk, too bad."

Ben was now thinking, even hoping, he was dreaming. "How do you know my name, and who are you?" Ben frantically searched for his cell phone to call the police, but remembered it was upstairs, and then sensed that the man was not a danger.

"My name isn't important," the man answered, "but my purpose for being here is. Your great-grandfather sent me, and I'm the Spirit of Leadership Past. We're going to look at some of the leadership principles that made AWSS great over time and, in the process, hopefully discover some of the things that went wrong, before my other two colleagues visit you this weekend."

*This can't be real*, Ben thought. He was pretty shaken but had trained himself not to show it. "And what if I don't want to hear what you have to say?" Ben asked. As soon as the words were out of his mouth, the spirit was standing next to him, but Ben never saw him move.

"Oh, you'll listen, all right. Because if you don't, any hope of your company being saved is pretty much gone forever," the spirit responded. "Now come join me on the couch, and try to control that mouth of yours."

With that, Ben walked over to the couch, but when he got there, the ghost was already back in his original place he had been when Ben first came down the stairs. "Now, I thought we would use your TV, if that's okay, to show you some scenes that will be helpful for you," the spirit explained.

"Oh, you're not going to transport me back to what you want to show me, like in Dickens' A *Christmas*

*Carol?*" Ben asked wryly.

"No need," the ghost answered with no trace of annoyance, "this is the 21st century and we can use technology to do what we used to do. It's a lot simpler." Then the spirit added, "It's so interesting that you are a 21st century CEO and you don't use much social media. Curious thing."

"I don't believe in . . ." Ben started to respond before the ghost interrupted. "Yes, I'm aware that you hate having to put yourself out there and do 'the Facebook,' as you call it. We'll address that later. Right now, I want to take you back and see if you can tell me where this is."

As Ben looked at the screen, he saw a group of people in what looked like a public park and recognized it immediately. It was called Holiday Park, and it was where his grandfather would host the AWSS family picnic every summer. The picnic was always a fun event, something Ben looked forward to every year.

"Do you recognize this?" the spirit asked.

"Of course," Ben answered, "it's Holiday Park, and that's the annual company picnic. Oh my, there's Bob Anderson, the company accountant, and my grandfather, my dad, Miriam, my brother Steven, and Charlie Mitchell, our operations guy, we're all there as we were every year."

"Very good," the spirit responded as if he was an elementary school teacher, "and what do you remember about that annual event?"

"Everyone was so glad to be there," Ben answered. "It was like a family reunion. My grandfather would walk around and he knew everyone by name. He would have gifts for all the kids and we would play games and have great food from a place in Englewood called Bistro to Go. It was a highlight of every summer."

"Yes, your great-grandfather, whom I believe you met earlier, founded that park with a grant from AWSS, which was located in Englewood at that time," the spirit reminded Ben. "That's why the picnic was there every year."

"My grandfather, and his father before him, always felt you should give back to the community," Ben reminisced. "That's why they lived there as well, wanting to have a community presence, someplace where we could all be grounded and known."

"Why was that important?" the spirit asked.

"The founders of AWSS felt like to be a community, you had to be part of a larger community," Ben answered. "They were also grateful for the support the community had given them, and they wanted to say thank you."

"Yes, but when you moved your offices to Manhattan, you sort of lost that sense of community, didn't you?" the ghost inquired.

"It had to be done," Ben said defensively. "We were going public on NASDAQ, and we needed to work among the big boys if we were going to play their game. It had to be done."

"We will have a chance to look at that decision in more detail later, but is there anything special about this picnic that we're viewing?" the ghost continued.

"Um, I look to be about 8 or 9, so I don't recall. I think it was the year my sister Miriam and I won the three-legged race, which was a big deal, but I doubt if that's what you are looking for," Ben laughed.

"That's right, but let's watch this next scene and see if it brings back memories," the spirit said.

On the screen, everyone was assembled in the park gazebo and Ben's grandfather was making an announcement. "I want to thank you all for coming today," said Ben's grandfather, "and especially all the families who are here. May I take this opportunity to thank you on behalf of AWSS for the sacrifices you have made and the commitment you have shown toward us this past year, which was one of our best years ever."

There was applause from the crowd, and some-one shouted out, "We love you, Mr. Holiday," to which Ben's grandfather responded, "I love you, too!"

"It has been my privilege," Ben's grandfather continued, "to lead this company as a second-generation Holiday, and it has been my hope to continue the wonderful tradition of family values and community service. God has been good to all of us, and we want to always share His blessings with as many of you as possible."

"Our company motto is, 'we protect your peace of mind,' and we have tried to live up to that motto with both our employees and our clients," Ben's grandfather continued. Several of AWSS' clients had representatives at the picnic, which was another tradition that allowed the AWSS team to meet those whose peace of mind they were protecting.

"I want to make an announcement today and that is that I'm stepping down as president of AWSS effective at the end of this year," Grandfather Holiday said, and when he did, a hush came over the exuberant picnic crowd.

"No, I'm not going anywhere," Grandfather explained, "so you won't be getting rid of me that easily. But effective at the end of this year, I'm turning the company over to my son, Albert, who will assume leadership of the day-to-day operations. I'll stay on in an advisory capacity, and I trust you'll give Al the same cooperation and assistance you have afforded me these many years."

Having said that, Grandfather Holiday called Albert forward and the crowd broke into spontaneous applause. Albert waved to the crowd, his family by his side, with Ben closest to him. "Thank you, Dad, and thanks to all of you for your faithful support of AWSS," Al said. "We could not do what we do without you. You give us peace of mind as we provide that for others, and I also want to thank you!"

After more applause, Grandfather Holiday distributed some prizes to the children present, recognized special milestones for some of the long-term employees, and then it was time to eat.

"That was a great day," Ben remembered. "My father was so happy."

"What else do you remember, anything?" the spirit asked.

"I remember what he said to me and Miriam, I think it was on the way home. He said he hoped to do the same thing for us that Grandfather had just done for him." Ben answered, with a bit of emotion in his voice.

"Yes, but he died before he could make that same presentation, and you took over the company with little time for transition," the spirit added.

"That's right, I went on to Dartmouth College to study business and came home to work toward becoming a CPA. I had so many ideas and was ready to change the world," Ben said wistfully. "Like my father before me, I didn't really want to work in the family business."

The spirit was ready to move on, however, and said, "Let's look at another clip and see what more we can learn and remember about AWSS' leadership past."

Ben was hoping to see more of the picnic, especially the replay of his and his sister's epic three-legged-race victory, but that was not to be. The next scene was a formal banquet setting at Rutgers, the State University of New Jersey. Ben remembered the day when his father received an honorary degree from Rutgers for his outstanding leadership efforts in the community, and for his generous contributions to Rutgers, his alma mater.

"Yes, I remember that day quite well too," Ben said without being asked. "That was such a great day for our family, and the last day we were all together. My sister was there, even though she was weak from chemo treatments," Ben said with more than a trace of sadness in his voice.

"Something else happened that day; you made a decision I believe," the spirit stopped to let Ben finish.

"Yes, it was that day I decided to one day run AWSS," Ben completed the spirit's thought.

"Why did you decide to do that?" the spirit asked.

"I thought I could make a significant contribution," Ben said with little emotion. "I had been in one of the big three accounting firms, and had been climbing the ladder, actually on my way to partnership, but it didn't feel right. I wanted to continue the family tradition, which hadn't been important to me up to that point. I was 37 and I was ready."

"Let's fast forward," the spirit suggested, and Ben could not believe what he saw. There were Ben and his family in a funeral home, but it wasn't his sister's funeral. It was for his father's.

"Oh my gosh," Ben exclaimed, "that was the biggest shock of my life. My dad wasn't supposed to die yet. It was a shock to all of us."

"How long had you been in the company by that time?" the ghost asked.

"About five years, I believe," Ben responded, "but things had already started to go downhill, and so it was time for me to step up and do the hard work."

"What kind of hard work?" the spirit asked, continuing his interrogation.

"I think you know," Ben said evasively, as he

continued to watch the funeral proceedings on the screen. "We had to lay some people off, we had to tighten things up. My dad had been too easy on some of the old timers, you know, emotionally attached to them, and we had to trim costs so we could compete in the global marketplace."

"Not to mention the decision you made behind everyone's back to enter into the domestic espionage business," the spirit said, filling in a portion of the story that Ben was omitting. "Tell me what you did and how you did it?" the visitor prodded Ben.

"You sound like that consultant I just had to let go," Ben snorted.

"In another life, I was a consultant," the spirit answered. "Now explain to me how you did it."

"I'd been with the company for about five years, and I was pretty agitated by what I had learned," Ben reported. "I had become CFO, and we had not turned a profit for a while. When Dad died, I fought to become the new CEO, and the board, who wanted to honor my dad and his legacy, decided to give me a chance."

"And what happened? Go on," the ghost urged Ben, who was becoming increasingly fidgety and nervous. Ben stood now and was pacing back and forth.

"Look, those things had to be done. Dad didn't have the stomach for it, but I did. I had no choice," Ben whined.

"And the decisions paid off in the long run," Ben told the spirit what he had gone over and rehearsed in his mind many times. "We cut costs, we got rid of the dead wood, and in five years, we went public on NASDAQ, and had moved our offices out of New Jersey into the City, where we were able to connect with a lot of new clients."

"Why did you personally move out of Englewood,

where your family had lived for generations?" the spirit asked.

"Simple," Ben shot back. "The taxes in New Jersey were ridiculous, so I picked up and moved to Connecticut. I had no ties to Englewood."

"That's interesting. Your family had been there for almost 100 years and you felt you had no ties. Is everything about the bottom line?" the spirit asked, to which he got no reply.

Suddenly, the TV screen went blank, and the spirit was holding a copy of the report that Francis had left and Jimmy had given to Ben, with the ultimatum that he read it or else Jimmy was gone.

"Where did you get that report?" Ben asked indignantly. "That's private and confidential."

"Your great-grandfather gave me a copy, and told me to make sure I read you portions of it," the spirit countered. "Let me read you the part about Ethics, which is what the first E stands for in L.E.A.D.E.R.S.

> Unfortunately, Ben Holiday has taken himself and AWSS down the slippery slope of unethical behavior. Although among his leadership team and employees he has those who would pursue the goal of acting ethically, Ben has squandered this asset. Ben has compromised the historic core values of AWSS, established at its founding by his great-grandfather and well-ingrained in the culture by the time Ben assumed the role of CEO. Those foundational principles included the notion that AWSS was like a family and all those who were employed there were considered to the company's most valuable resource.
>
> Qualities such as integrity, compassion, transparency, and most importantly,

*inclusion, were all practiced by Ben's prede-
cessors. Employees at all levels were treated
ethically and, as a result, their loyalty and
commitment to the vision, mission, and success
of AWSS were strong and resolute. Ben's predecessors constantly communicated formally and
informally with employees and were transparent about the company's financial status.*

Ben winced as he heard the indictment on the
company's leadership, which in his mind was one and
the same with who he was. The spirit stopped reading
and gazed intently at Ben, who was sitting on the couch,
the look of a defeated man on his face for just a moment.
Then Ben was quickly back on the attack, defending his
decisions.

"All that's water under the bridge, a dead past that
can't be revived," Ben said dismissively. "The community
service, the family environment, the commitment to service, it's different now. Business isn't what it used to be
when Grandpa and his team did their work. I made hard
choices, and I would do it all again."

"Would you really, Ben, knowing what you know
today?" the spirit responded, seemingly surprised by
Ben's sudden hardening.

"Business is about the bottom line. If we don't
have profits, we cannot do the things that we once did."
Ben was on the attack, lecturing the spirit.

"Yet you did have profits when you first took
over, and you still cut staff, training, travel, and IT investment—except for your pet project," the spirit shot back.
"It seems that you cut the company off from the very life
energy that had served it well for 100 years."

"That's your opinion, which is why I don't think this
report is worth the time and money we contributed to
make it happen," Ben said with disgust. "You consultants

just don't get it."

With that, the screen came back to life and Ben was looking at a familiar face, that of Charlie Mitchell, former head of operations at AWSS. "There's old Charlie," Ben said with a smile.

"Yes, whatever became of Charlie?" the spirit asked. "He was with AWSS for many years."

"I lost track of Charlie after we moved and I moved," Ben said sheepishly, leaving out part of the story.

"You mean you lost track of him after you let him go?" the spirit asked, already knowing the answer.

"Look, that had to be done. He wasn't doing the job, and people were covering for him because he wasn't producing," Ben said with a furrow in his forehead, voice raised. "We let him go along with his son, Martin, who also wasn't producing, and I don't know what became of them. We aren't running a social service agency. I'm sure they did just fine." Ben mentioned nothing of their falling out over the domestic surveillance program.

"How can you be so sure?" the spirit inquired. "But enough of that for now, my time with you is almost over." Ben looked at the clock and it was 3:38 AM; they had been at this for a while, longer than Ben thought.

"I can't stay but the report will be here to guide you through the rest of the story of the leadership past in AWSS. Here are some of the highlights that include a look at AWSS' corporate governing values. How well do you think you've been living by or maintaining those, Ben?" Things such as:

- Placing people before profit;
- Having a meaningful community presence;
- Providing excellence in product and services;
- Delivering innovative technologies that serve our clients' interests;

- Creating peace of mind for employees and clients.

"That's what AWSS stood for, but that's no longer true," the spirit explained. "You maintain that those things had to go and are no longer relevant as business strategies or a source of competitive advantage. The report argues that you did away with those things and cut the company off from what some would call their spiritual roots," the spirit explained dispassionately. Ben remembered what his great-grandfather said, that he had been overseeing the company all along through the vision and company values.

"Tomorrow night, another consultant will visit you, the Spirit of Leadership Present, and that spirit will give you a real behind-the-scenes look at AWSS. My time is finished, good-bye. Thanks for the beer." Ben had not paid attention, but the spirit had consumed a six-pack of Heineken while they talked. *Boy, those spirits get thirsty*, Ben thought.

With that, Ben woke up from his sleep, and the clock said 4:15 AM. Ben jumped out of bed and ran down to the TV room, where he found things pretty much as he left them earlier, except for one thing. There were now two copies of the consultant's report, where there had only been the one he brought home. As Ben opened the pages, some of the portions of the second report were highlighted in yellow, and were initialed "SLP."

Ben considered the initials, but did not want to believe they stood for Spirit of Leadership Past.

*This has been a strange night*, Ben said to himself, *but apparently I wasn't dreaming. Or maybe I had two reports, one inside the other that I brought home from the office*, Ben reasoned, trying to convince himself that the second report he held in his hand didn't really come from his nighttime visitor, but in his heart, he knew it did.

# Act Three

Ben reflected on his middle-of-the-night encounter, thinking back most of Saturday to the scenes the spirit had shown him on his TV screen. Those led to other vivid memories of his past, in which AWSS had always played a leading part. He remembered the times his dad would bring people home from the company for dinner, and his mom never complained, but was always ready to set another place at the table.

Ben remembered the phone ringing, then eventually his dad's beeper going off, to notify his dad that someone could not take their security shift. If there was no one else to replace him (or her), then his dad would go out and do it himself, even if it was the night shift. And yes, there were "hers" in the company serving as security guards, for AWSS was among the first to employ women guards on the night shift, so they could support their families and be home in time to see the children off to school. When Ben graduated from high school, and then Dartmouth, some of the staff, including Charlie Mitchell and his wife, were present, representing the company and celebrating with Ben's family.

Then there were the stories of his grandfather and great-grandfather that he had heard regularly when he was growing up. There were stories about the faith they had to launch new risky ventures, things like the private investigation division, the government and international divisions, and the home security systems, long before those went mainstream. Ben's grandfathers were entrepreneurial, but they were also giants in the community.

Ben's great-grandfather had founded Holiday Park, where the annual picnic was held. When Englewood needed a library, his grandfather had made the first grant to start one, and then worked tirelessly to raise the rest of the money from the community to make it a reality. It carried the family name, Holiday Public Library, in honor of his grandfather's efforts. They had sponsored Little League teams and then soccer teams so they could buy uniforms and play on the baseball and soccer fields at Holiday Park. His family, through AWSS, had established a summer jobs program for local youth and did a Christmas program to provide gifts for the less fortunate in the community.

While Ben admired his family's efforts, it always bothered him that they did all this at the expense of what they as a family, and as the founders, could have taken out of the company for themselves. They all lived in modest homes, although in Englewood there was nothing like modest property taxes. There was a big world right across the river, just a drive across the bridge to New York City, but the family refused to get involved there, choosing instead to make its mark in little Englewood rather than in the big city. Yes, they had some clients in the City, but they never even went to a baseball game over there!

That's why Ben chose to study accounting and

finance at Dartmouth, wanting to specialize in corporate finance. Ben did his senior project on what it would take for AWSS to go public and be listed on the New York Stock Exchange. Ben did not want to work for the company right after graduation, and his father supported that decision, wanting Ben to work at other places to see how those companies did business, and to make sure that if Ben wanted to work at AWSS, it was something he really wanted to do.

As time went on, Ben could not help but think that he could take the company to the next level, which would include an initial public offering to raise capital for expansion into high tech security systems. When Ben finally entered the business, it was naturally in the accounting department, where he quickly rose through the ranks to become CFO. He wasn't CFO for quite nine months when his father had a stroke, which put him in a coma for three weeks before he passed away at the age of 67.

It is true that Ben had worked behind the scenes, telling very few people about the controversial domestic spying technology and partnership with the government. After 9/11, the new Department of Homeland Security was interested in paying closer attention to what its own citizens and residents were saying and doing, and Ben saw an opportunity to get involved in this work. After all, there were 300 million Americans, and they all had cell phones.

Ben had circumvented all the normal company protocols, and worked with outside agencies to develop and then employ the spying program and technology. When the story broke in the media, AWSS was named as an accomplice in the program and all hell literally broke loose. The company lost customers and revenue and Ben was constantly on the defensive to justify his decision to get involved.

Charlie Mitchell found out about the program before it went public and had vehemently disagreed with the direction Ben was headed. That is in part why Ben had to let him go—to try and keep a lid on the program. It was true that Charlie was slipping and up in years, but Ben mostly wanted him out of the way so that the surveillance program could proceed without opposition. When the rest of the team found out about the surveillance program, they were flabbergasted and irate, arguing that this in no way represented the company's values, nor did it coincide with the company's purpose statement:

> AWSS exists to provide companies and institutions with peace of mind that their property and business interests are secure while providing a world-class place of employment for all AWSS security personnel.

Ben did all this thinking while he ran his Saturday errands, which included some basic Christmas shopping. Ben had no family except for his brother's and sister's families, so he had few gifts to buy. He would go to his brother's home for Christmas and wanted to have a few things to bring with him on that day. Ben had been too busy with work over the years to think much about a family of his own, and he also felt the Holidays had probably taken the company as far as it could go.

His nephew Jimmy was not a Holiday since he carried his sister's married name of Matthews. Ben didn't believe Jimmy had what it took to lead the company, and, in all probability, Jimmy would depart when Ben did not comply with his demand to read the report, which Ben still did not intend to do. He would not be bullied by his nephew or some crazy dreams to do what he didn't want to do. As the day went on, Ben dug his heels in, refusing to acknowledge his role in the company's troubles.

By the time Ben had run his errands and stopped to get something to eat, it was 4 PM. He was watching the clock, in a way dreading the night ahead, but also trying to drag out his out-of-house duties so he would not have to read that blasted report. He knew the "consultant" or whoever he was that was in his dream had wanted him to reconnect with his company's history, but if he or anyone thought they were going to get him to second guess the way he had led the company over the last ten years, they were sadly mistaken.

Ben got home at 6:30 PM and had some loads of laundry to do. He also wanted to watch the Knicks on TV that night, and then catch the Giants football game tomorrow before the Packers-Bears game on Sunday night. Sports were Ben's main outlet for recreation, and he went to as many basketball and hockey games as possible. The NFL was better suited to armchair watching, which is why he had invested so much into his entertainment system. He had stopped to pick up a pizza for dinner, and he sat down at 8 PM to watch the Knicks play the Bulls in Chicago.

The Knicks lost by eight, and before Ben went to bed, he made sure all the doors were locked. For good measure, he unplugged the television, even disconnecting the cable cord, just to make sure that no one—or no thing—could interrupt his sleep on this particular night. Ben went to get a Heineken; he had put plenty in the fridge after the spirit had cleaned him out the night before. *How could a dream consultant drink my beer?* Ben thought, but refused to find an answer, still choosing to believe it was all indeed a dream. As he was heading to his bedroom, however, he noticed the consultant's report, in fact both copies, sitting on his coffee table.

He picked them up and headed upstairs to get ready for bed.

After his bedtime prep routine, he settled into bed and thumbed through the pages. This time he got further than before when he threw the report across the room. He did not like what he was reading, but he didn't want another nighttime visitor either, so he pressed on, jumping around and reading certain portions that caught his attention.

For the first time, he took the time to read the introduction, which was an explanation of the acronym L.E.A.D.E.R.S. Ben had to admit that he had spent so much time on what he called the hard issues of the business, things like technology, finance, and strategy, that he had totally neglected the softer issues of leadership and management. He had been so focused on the business that he had neglected to pay attention to the *people* inside the business, or outside of it, for that matter.

*Maybe, just maybe, there was something to this L.E.A.D.E.R.S. stuff,* Ben thought for the first time, *but at the same time, they don't understand the nuances of going public or the realities of the new world of security after 9/11.* Ben was stubbornly clinging to his flimsy rationale for what he had done and where he had taken the business.

Ben felt he was making progress because this time, he didn't toss the report against the wall. He wasn't ready to subscribe to the report's prognosis or cure, but he was finally open to what it had to say. Ben flipped back and forth between Francis' report, and the highlighted one that his Friday night visitor had left with him. His eyes caught a highlighted passage under "decision making":

> *As President and CEO of AWSS, Ben Holiday uses his position to make all decisions relative to business development, delivery of security*

*services, finance, equipment purchases, em-
ployee policies, and employee hiring and firing.
All managers and supervisors essentially do
Ben's bidding, having little if any influence in the
way day-to-day operations are carried out.*

Ben read that and thought, *What's wrong with
that? That's what I'm getting paid to do—make decisions.
My head is better than all the rest of the heads put together,
so where's the problem?* Smug and satisfied that he was
correct in dismissing the report as so much trendy jargon,
Ben did a quick channel flip with the remote from his
bed before he turned off the TV and went to bed. The
last time he looked at his clock, it was 11:25 PM.

Ben was sound asleep when suddenly he was
awakened by more sounds coming from his TV room
downstairs. *It can't be,* he thought, *not again, not tonight.*
He remembered the words of the previous night's visitor that someone else would visit him tonight, a second
consultant, but he had dismissed that, not wanting to
focus on the possibility.

Now he could not ignore it any longer. He stayed
in bed, straining to hear what was going on downstairs
for a clue of what was in store for him when he finally
went down. Whoever it was had obviously reconnected
the TV and something was playing that sounded like
a war movie, with bombs going off and machine guns
firing.

Finally, Ben could stand it no longer, so he put
on his sweat pants and sweatshirt and ventured downstairs. The first thing he noticed was that there was
not just one visitor, but two. *Oh, good grief,* he thought,
*someone sent a committee! They're trying to outnumber
me!* The next thing he saw was the television, which was
still unplugged and disconnected as far as he could tell.
Even so, there was something playing on the screen, as if

everything was still attached. The visitors were actually eating popcorn and drinking what Ben presumed to be his Heineken.

When Ben came down the stairs, both visitors looked up, without getting off the couch. One was an older man, probably in his early fifties, dressed in a jacket and dress shirt without a tie. The second was a much younger man, probably in his twenties, dressed casually in jeans and a long-sleeved t-shirt. They were watching the movie *Patton*, one of Ben's favorites, but Ben could not tell where the movie was coming from, for the DVD and TV were not even plugged in.

Ben was the first to speak, "Who are you guys, and what are you doing drinking my beer and making yourself at home in my TV room?" Ben asked, certain he was going to be amused by their answers. "And, how are you able to use my TV?"

"My name is the Spirit of Leadership Present," the older man replied, "and this is my apprentice who is here to meet you. He's heard so much about you. We bring our own power, by the way, so all we need is a screen to show you what we have come to reveal," the spirit explained. "We know you like this movie and feel that it represents the kind of leader you have aspired to be."

"How have you heard so much about me?" Ben asked, deciding to play along but not yet convinced this wasn't another dream. Ben picked up his remote control and pressed the buttons, but nothing changed and the movie continued.

"We often use you as an example of poor leadership in our training sessions," the lead spirit responded. "That's why my apprentice has been anxious to meet you." The apprentice said nothing, but shook his head enthusiastically.

"So I'm the poster child for poor leadership?" Ben

asked while sitting down on the chair opposite the two visitors. "I'm sure there are worse examples than I."

"Uh, not really," the spirit responded. "You pretty much are a bad example of every aspect included in our L.E.A.D.E.R.S. acronym." Once again, the apprentice enthusiastically nodded his head in agreement.

"Come on, you guys," Ben shot back. "That's ridiculous. Look at all I did. I took the company public, I moved our offices into the City, I cut expenses, I . . ." but before Ben could finish, the lead visitor interrupted.

"Yes, we're here to talk to you about those expenses you cut, to show you the results of those so-called strategic decisions," the spirit explained. "That's what's playing on the screen now if you care to watch."

Suddenly the scene shifted on the TV from the movie *Patton* to a scene of an old man sitting in front of a television, watching another old war movie. As Ben watched, the view shifted from behind the man who was watching to the front where Ben could see the man's face.

"It's Charlie, Charlie Mitchell" Ben exclaimed. "Good old Charlie. He always was a war buff."

"Yes, he was a veteran and enjoyed watching war movies," the spirit said. "That's pretty much all he does now."

"Yeah, I lost track of Charlie after . . .," Ben stopped short of finishing his sentence.

"After the downsizing you mean?" the spirit finished the statement for Ben.

"Yes, after we cut costs to be more competitive." Ben preferred his version to the spirit's.

"Charlie had put in 37 years with AWSS," the spirit said. "What did you do for his transition out of the company?"

"I'm not sure," Ben replied sheepishly. "We were

busy and I just had HR take care of all that. We gave him what he had coming to him."

"Really?" the spirit said in disbelief. "You really think he got what was coming to him?" The spirit shook his head slowly.

"I think we gave him a two-month severance, and I gifted him some stock when we went public," Ben said defensively.

"Yes, two months for 37 years, after you gave him 15 minutes to vacate his office. No party, no recognition, no chance to tie up loose ends," the spirit said with a trace of sadness in his voice. "He had known your grand-father and served your father faithfully." Then the spirit added, "And we all know what happened to the stock once the company ran into trouble."

Ben couldn't watch the TV any longer, for Charlie looked old and pitiful sitting in a wheelchair.

"Do you know where Charlie is right now?" the spirit inquired.

"No," Ben said softly, "I told you I lost touch with him."

"He is in a county rest home in Bergen County, not far from where you grew up," the spirit informed Ben. "The conditions are poor, and he spends his days watching TV programs he can't hear or understand. That's his reward for over 37 years of faithful service."

"That's not my fault," Ben snapped. "He should have prepared better for his retirement. He has family. Why aren't they helping? I'm not my brother's keeper!"

When he said that, the spirit, his apprentice and Ben, all sat in stunned silence. Ben had used the term "brother's keeper," and they all knew that was one of the values Ben's grandfather had instilled in the company, and one by which his father had lived and run AWSS.

Ben tried to regain his composure, but he was

caught by his own words. "I had no choice. I had to cut costs. Investors were breathing down my neck. We weren't getting the results from Charlie, and I had to make a change."

"Results? You weren't getting results?" the spirit said, his voice rising with each word. "You wanted results, but you wanted them on your terms. If you wanted results, you would have kept Tommy Morris as your head of business development. But when Tommy opposed the direction you had chosen, you let him *and* Charlie go."

When the spirit mentioned Tommy's name, the TV came back on and there was a scene at another company in what looked like its board or conference room. The team looked like it was engaged in intense discussion. At the head of the table sat none other than Tommy Morris, AWSS' former head of business development.

When Ben looked more closely at the scene, he saw Francis, the consultant he had relieved of his duties, who was working with Tommy and the team of people gathered in the room.

"Tommy was young and idealistic. He had good ideas, but they didn't make business sense," Ben said, trying to head off where the conversation was going.

The spirit confronted Ben with the truth: "So you let him go and he went over to your biggest competitor where he is now taking them to the next level of productivity and profitability. What were those business ideas that were so radical and unrealistic?" the spirit asked Ben.

Ben said quietly, "I don't remember," while staring down at the floor and then glancing at the TV screen, where Francis was doing what Ben assumed he had wanted to do for AWSS.

"I think you do," the spirit said, pressing Ben as a prosecuting attorney would do.

"It was something about communication and coming into the 21st century where the treatment of people and building teams were concerned," Ben said. "It was all soft stuff, but I wasn't going to do 'the Facebook thing,' no matter what Tommy said. It was irrelevant to our business plan."

Ben had always referred to any new initiative to connect people in the business or any people development issue as "the Facebook thing." He had no time for such foolishness, and made sure the company didn't either.

"So what was Tommy recommending that you do? What did he see as the problems at AWSS?" the spirit asked, continuing his cross examination.

"Tommy said that not enough people were involved in the decision making of the company. He felt the communications were what he called 'top down,'" Ben stated. "He said my decision to get involved in the expansion of our surveillance capabilities was a colossal mistake, and unethical as well." It was the first time that Ben had mentioned the domestic spying initiative with any of the visiting spirits.

"I thought you didn't remember why he left?" the spirit said, but Ben did not respond.

"But all that's not the reason I let Tommy go," Ben said. "He was a screw up, always late for our early morning meetings, and he had ideas but no wherewithal to pull them off. He also wanted to invest more in the development of the staff, but I was against it. Tommy just didn't fit with our corporate culture," Ben continued, satisfied that he had refuted any accusations that he had done the wrong thing by letting Tommy go.

"Do you know why Tommy was always late?" the spirit asked. At that, the apprentice sat straight up in his seat, and Ben had almost forgotten that he was present in the room, since he said nothing.

"What's wrong with your apprentice?" Ben asked, trying to change the direction of the conversation. "He doesn't say much."

It was then that the apprentice said something in sign language to his older counterpart. The spirit interpreted for Ben and said, "My young apprentice is deaf and mute, so he can't say anything, but he's recording our discussion for future reference."

"Recording? What? Where? With what?" Ben demanded to know.

"Right over there," the spirit pointed to a small camera next to the TV. "I told you that we've been studying you for quite some time, and want to use this video for training purposes for our other consultants. You're a classic example of what *not* to do while leading a company!" the spirit pointed out to Ben.

"I don't know how I feel about that, and what's more, I feel like my privacy has been invaded," Ben complained.

"Isn't that what your surveillance program does to other people, Mr. Holiday?" the spirit countered. "How does it feel to have the tables turned to have someone spy on you?"

Ben stopped short of responding, for he was no fool, and knew that the program, *his* program, had cost the company dearly. *This guy may use the recording against me in the future, so I had better shut up*, Ben reasoned.

"Tommy was opposed to that program," the spirit continued, "but you saw that it had great potential for growth and increased revenue, so you overrode his concerns and pressed on."

Ben nodded, but decided to say nothing, fearing he had already said too much. "In fact, that was the focus of the business program you were watching on TV last night if I remember correctly," the spirit went on without Ben's participation.

"When the story hit about your espionage program, some of your oldest clients left you because they were concerned that your guards and systems were actually spying on them. Tommy confronted you on this issue before it became public and that's why you let him go," the spirit said dispassionately. "But you never answered my question as to why Tommy was always late. Do you know why?"

"I don't, and don't much care," Ben said at that point, pursing his lips into a frown.

The TV turned on again, and Ben saw a home where a young boy seemed to be on a rampage. He was throwing things, kicking doors, and at one point smashed a computer monitor in his anger. A man, woman, and young girl were chasing him, eventually holding him down while the boy screamed, a flow of obscenities streaming from his lips.

"Is that Tommy?" Ben asked, knowing that it was.

"Yes, that's the frequent scene at Tommy's home, Mr. Holiday," the spirit responded. "Tommy has a special needs son, and his presence was often required at home to help his wife calm the boy when he was agitated."

"I didn't know," Ben said. "Why didn't he tell me? I don't think anyone knew."

"Oh, everyone else knew. He tried to tell you, but you wouldn't listen, you wouldn't give him a chance to explain," the spirit explained. "He didn't want to lose his job. Others on your team knew, but didn't want to bring it up to you, since you seldom had time or interest in such as you called them, 'personal matters.'"

Ben watched as much of the home scene as he could, but it was painful to see such turmoil in anyone's home.

"When you let him go, with your customary speech, 'You have 15 minutes to vacate the premises. Empty your desk with our head of security watching and when you leave and turn in your pass, we'll give you your two-week severance check,' Tommy and his family went through some tough times," the spirit said. "It's interesting that you were spying on all those people and knew their secrets but you didn't know the secrets of those who were sharing an office with you." The apprentice signed something to his mentor, but the spirit did not tell Ben what it was.

"Until Tommy landed with his new company, they could not keep their son in the special program he needed, and thus they lost some of the progress the boy had made in school," the spirit reported. "Tommy and his wife actually split up, with Tommy leaving the house to try and get his life back together and look for a new job. I'm happy to report that they're back together, but the son continues to suffer in his school program that is less than adequate for the son's needs."

"I'm sorry to hear that, I truly am," Ben stumbled for words. "I didn't know, no one told me, no one told me," Ben's tone softened as he kept saying, "No one told me."

The apprentice signed and this time the spirit interpreted. "My young apprentice says that you have to learn to read people, just like I had to learn to read my young friend's signing. He also said that all the signs were there, but you just didn't read them." The apprentice was obviously pleased that he had contributed, and he saw that his mentor had accurately interpreted his thoughts to Ben.

"I thought he was deaf?" Ben said sarcastically. "How did he know what I said?"

The spirit responded, "You have heard of reading

lips, haven't you, Mr. Holiday?"

"So let's summarize, Mr. Holiday," the lead spirit continued, "our time is running out and so is yours. Here is an additional overview of the present state of your leadership, and I'm quoting from the MCC report."

> Ben's top-down leadership style and just-do-it personality have weakened the organization to the point of collapse. To Ben, resilience is simply "suck it up" so he tells employees to "deal with it" when it comes to facing the company's adversity. Ben has no clue that when he made the unilateral decisions to engage the domestic surveillance initiative, it led to a tremendous loss of company morale. When confronted with this reality, Ben responded to his leadership team's pushback by firing Tommy and several of his co-workers who voiced strong disapproval over the domestic surveillance initiative.

> Despite this lack of understanding and resilience-building by Ben, there is a surprising level of individual resiliency among a number of AWSS employees. These folks have "stuck with it," even though the work environment Ben has created does not encourage such behaviors. This is no doubt a combination of personal qualities and the remnant of commitment to AWSS that remains in them that was instilled by the positive leadership of Ben's predecessors.

> How can AWSS build the kind of organizational resilience that is necessary for it to again achieve the type of missional and financial success that was the case under Ben's predecessors? It's going to be a great challenge. Since so much of the responsibility of creating the capacity of resilience among employees

*typically falls on the leaders, AWSS will struggle to make any progress in this area. Ben does not reflect the qualities of a leader who is resilient and who can encourage and develop resilience in others at AWSS. As stated previously in this section, leaders who are positive and optimistic, and who are supportive and reassuring, use these practices and behaviors to build resilience among those who they lead.*

*Consequently, for AWSS to be more resilient, Ben needs to change, which is a common theme throughout this report. Ben must realize the importance of having a resilient organization and understand that for this to exist, resilience must begin with him. He needs to consider all of the previous discussion regarding the L.E.A.D.E.R.S. Model and how his shortcomings in these areas impact his ability to develop resilience in himself and for AWSS. Since Resilience is the sixth practice in the Model, we strongly advise Ben that he heed the recommendations in the previous five steps. As he does that, employees will respond to his efforts and the changes they see, and the organization will hopefully find new reservoirs of resilience to help AWSS survive and thrive.*

Ben listened passively to the list of his leadership sins and looked at the clock. It was 4:19 AM, and this had turned into one of the longest nights of his life. He had abandoned any hope that this was only a dream hours ago.

"One final thing, Mr. Holiday. You're perhaps surprised by our existence, but you should not be," the spirit explained. "There has been a spirit at AWSS and it was the founding vision of your great-grandfather. We are its caretakers. When you got away from the vision of the organization, you got yourself into trouble." The spirit read the vision aloud for Ben to hear:

> *AWSS exists to provide companies and institutions with peace of mind because their property and business interests are secure while providing a world-class place of employment for all AWSS security personnel.*

"It's time to get back to that vision, Mr. Holiday, if you're serious about saving your company. You've done everything but provide your clients with peace of mind."

"Mr. Holiday," the spirit was looking to conclude. "Mr. Holiday?" he repeated when Ben did not respond because he was lost in thought. "Do you have any questions?"

"Yes, I do," Ben responded, and the spirits who had been ready to depart, sat back in their chairs, surprised at this most recent response, for Ben seldom asked anyone for input or their opinion.

---

The spirits, who were ready to go out the door with their coats on, sat back down in their chairs, stunned that Ben had questions. They were skeptical, having studied Ben over the years as a model of bad leadership who only asked questions that could help him get his way.

"I don't understand the connection between what you're showing me and the condition of our company," Ben asked, implying once again that the company's problems were not his fault. "We've done a good job at what we've accomplished and provided the best of service that we knew how to deliver."

The spirits looked at one another, shocked by this most recent development. "Excuse us, Mr. Holiday, if we're a little taken aback," the lead spirit said. "We weren't prepared for any questions from you, but we'll be glad to answer. In your pursuit of lower costs, you gutted the company, not of workers, but of *skilled* leaders and managers, people who could continue the tradition that you referred to—of excellence and service."

"You also made decisions on your own, without considering that others may have a different perspective on them from an ethical and even practical point of view," the spirit paused to let Ben process what he had said.

The young apprentice signed something to the elder, and he nodded his head in agreement. "My young friend wants me to remind you that taking care of your team members is being loyal to the true spirit of this company, the spirit of your great-grandfather whom you met during his visit last night. A company's vision is just like us—a spirit that you can sense and feel but can't touch."

"That vision is the real spirit of AWSS, and you violated it when you stopped sharing and caring," but before the spirit could finish, Ben interrupted.

"Sharing and caring? Bah humbug!" Ben retorted. "You sound like something from Sesame Street and not from Wall Street. Sharing and caring? I only care about profits and of sharing them with those who help me earn them!" Ben felt a resurgence of his usual surliness coming forth.

"Really?" the spirit replied. "You share profits with those who help you? Is that what Charlie Mitchell would say? Is that the story of Tommy Morris?" the spirit was on a roll. "I could name you six others who were marginalized in their role at AWSS or eliminated altogether because of your drive to cut expenses. And how has that worked for you, now that your company's being dragged through the mud on national television?" With this comment, the TV came back on, this time showing the news clip that Ben had watched on the business channel the night before.

"You don't understand the first thing . . .," Ben began, but this time the spirit interrupted.

"No, *you* don't get it," the spirit snapped. "Not only did you cut the heart out of the company, you cut it off from its community base. You moved the company to New York, and you severed all ties with those things that your grandfathers and father held dear—the library, the park, the annual company picnic, the employee assistance plans—all gone in the interest of profit." The spirit stopped, surprised at his own passion and anger as he ticked off the list of cuts Ben had made.

Ben was back on the defensive and said, "I wasn't alone in those decisions, my board was with me in them all."

"Your board? You mean your yes men!" the spirit shot back. "You handpicked those people and paid them a fee to tell you what you wanted to hear. You forced those off the board who had decided to give you a chance to honor your family's legacy. You gave the new members stock in the company, and they thought they had struck it rich. Now that stock is worthless, thanks to you and your board."

Once again, the young mentor signed something to his mentor with great urgency. "Oh yes, my assistant wants me to remind you that you removed the picture of your great-grandfather that was in your board room and replaced it with white boards and a projector screen. You substituted technology for the heart and spirit of the company, which was its mission and its leadership."

Ben had never given that change a second thought, figuring they needed the wall space in the room for their meetings and analysis. He wasn't even sure where those pictures were.

"You have been agonizing, Ben, over the revenue of AWSS, but your real problem is that you cut yourself off from the company's vision. In your pursuit of Wall Street, you lost your way and you've reaped what you've sown."

"I don't get it," Ben said wistfully. "I thought I was doing things in the best interests of the company," but then he let his words trail off.

"You failed to see how *taking care of your people* was doing something that was in the best interests of the company," the spirit explained with emphasis, the young apprentice nodding in agreement. "Look at what Tommy has done for your competitor. He has brought innovation, a sense of team and purpose, and they are cleaning your clock in the marketplace."

Ben did not want to acknowledge what they were saying, so he shook his head and said, "No, you're wrong. It was just bad luck, a matter of being in the wrong place at the wrong time. We'll be back, we'll turn it around." With those words, the spirits got up to leave.

"Don't bother seeing us out," they said. "We know the way since we've been here many times before." Ben was too worn out to ask them what they meant. They continued, "You'll have another visitor tomorrow night, the Spirit of Leadership Future, to show you the full ramifications of your decisions unless you change course. You have a lot to think about, Ben. It's not too late, but it almost is."

With that, Ben awakened and sat straight up in bed. Looking at his watch, it was 5:29 AM on the Sunday before Christmas. Ben got out of bed and started to read in earnest the report Francis and great-grandfather Fred had given him, and then he intuitively knew what he had to do before his next visitor came to call that night.

# Act Four

Ben drank his morning coffee but did not go online to check his emails. He did not go out to get the Sunday paper. He sat at his small kitchen table with the consultant's report in front of him, both copies. He determined to read as much as he could handle, and then he had a trip to make. It was Sunday, the Giants were playing the Redskins in Washington, D.C. so he could make a trip and there would not be much traffic.

He felt humiliated and condemned as he read, but he was still apprehensive that Francis, who had only spent one week with him, could have that much of a handle on AWSS' problems. At this point in the weekend, however, he was ready to read, if only to keep his mind off the events and visitors of Friday and Saturday nights.

The report continued:

> Ben needs to understand what these values meant in the day-to-day operation of AWSS, the values that were imprinted on the culture of AWSS. He must realize that these values were not only "right" in principle, but understand why they worked—why AWSS became

successful as a result of grounding its business on these values.

Next, Ben must own these cherished values for himself. They cannot just be "words on a poster" that are displayed on a wall. He must embody them. He has to begin the process of changing his perspective—what he considers to be ethical and unethical—which then can lead to a shift in his attitude and, hopefully, a change in his behavior. As this happens, it's important that Ben communicate to his leadership team and employees that it will no longer be "business as usual" at AWSS, that this internal change regarding his ethical view of things is changing and explain why this is happening. However, words alone will not make a difference. It's essential that Ben begin modeling this changing ethical perspective through his behavior. And while Ben shows the way, he must also let those at AWSS know what these new ethical expectations are for everyone.

Ben also needs to listen to others in his organization when it comes to establishing and maintaining ethical standards of behavior. In most cases, companies include individuals who represent a collection of beliefs and commitments in determining what is the "right and wrong" thing to do. As Ben develops his own ethical perspectives and begins to change how he sees things ethically, it will be very helpful for him to consider what employees at AWSS think. This process of listening to others will create a sort of "collective reasoning" among Ben, his leadership team, and staff members, leading to a greater buy-in to establishing ethical standards, *attitudes, and behaviors that can be more easily and consistently implemented.*

Ben was open to the reality, perhaps for the first time, that he had tried too hard to make AWSS *his* company, to make his personal mark and continue the family legacy his way. He had always denied that pressure was there to succeed as his fathers had done before him, but it was ever before him, looming over him like a cloud—at least in his mind. He had wanted to instill his vision and along the way lost sight of *the* vision, the one that was established in the company when it started. In trying to overcome his insecurities as a leader, he pretended like they were not there.

Then there was the issue of the domestic surveillance. He thought it was lucrative and it would help the bottom line, which was what Ben had always sought to do. As a finance and accounting student, Ben had been taught to focus on the bottom line, and it had worked for him while his father was running the company. The problems came in when Ben became the lead man. He needed to expand his repertoire of leadership and management skills, but he had continued to rely on his finance background.

The report quoted the famous saying, "To a hammer, every problem looks like nail." Ben had treated every problem as a profit problem (or opportunity), and he had totally ignored other business issues. Ben actually grabbed a tablet and took some notes, not wanting to forget what he was thinking as he read through some of the report. He took one sheet of paper and down the left hand column he wrote the letters L.E.A.D.E.R.S., using the entire length of the page so that he could write some notes next to each letter.

He filled one page and then another with his thoughts, and before he knew it, it was almost 11 AM.

65

He got dressed and wanted to get on the road for his trip. On the way, he stopped to grab a quick burger and chocolate shake, and headed for the George Washington Bridge. He brought along his note tablet and the reports to work on when he got where he was going.

* * *

As he had hoped, Ben found Sunday traffic to be light as he headed down the Connecticut Turnpike toward New York. He navigated his way around the city to the George Washington Bridge, and then headed into New Jersey to familiar territory. The weather was sunny and warmer than usual for the time of year. Christmas was only a few days away, and he saw evidence of the season with decorations all along the way. He never put up decorations in his own home, for it took precious time away from his work and his attendance, usually by himself, to many sporting events.

There it was, the *Welcome to Englewood* sign that indicated Ben was back home. Traffic was still light as he continued through the town square to the place where he had so many childhood memories—Holiday Park. When he arrived, he saw young men and some boys on the basketball courts playing hoops.

Ben parked the car and got out to stroll the grounds, but he was shocked and saddened by what he saw. The tennis courts had no nets. He was hoping it was just because it was winter, but the court lines were faded and the playing surface was badly cracked. He continued his walk and noticed that the trash containers had not been emptied for quite a while, so soggy litter was everywhere. He walked back over to the basketball courts and there were no nets on the rims. In fact, one of the rims was bent downward at a 30-degree angle, rendering it useless.

Ben then walked toward the place of his greatest

childhood triumph—the field where he and his sister had won the three-legged race at the company picnic. It didn't look nearly as big as it did on that memorable race day. Off to the side was what Ben remembered to be a massive pavilion, but now boards nailed across the steps and signs prevented anyone from entering. He could picture his grandfather when he turned the company over to his father in that very place. Now that place was unusable.

Ben sat on one of the benches that wasn't covered with bird droppings or didn't have a board or a screw jutting out of it. He noticed a few people walking their dogs along the asphalt paths that were also in disrepair. Ben had so many good memories here, but that was a lifetime ago. He looked over at the sign that was hanging on a chain link fence at the park entrance, and it read "Holiday Park: Presented by the Grateful Founders of Always Watching Security Services to the People of Englewood." Ben knew that's what the sign indicated, but the graffiti and weather wear almost made the sign unreadable, which Ben determined was just as well.

As Ben reflected on the previous 48 hours since he had left the office on Friday, he came to one conclusion: The visiting consultants were correct in their assessment that he had not been faithful to the founders' spirit of AWSS. His great-grandfather, who had visited him on Friday night, had every right to be angry. The mission had gotten away from Ben. In fact, everything, including the bottom line, had proved to be elusive, and Ben sat there thinking, *This park is indicative of the company's condition. It's in shambles and its day has passed.*

Yet, Ben looked around and concluded, *There is nothing here that can't be fixed and restored. With a little money and a lot of heart and vision, this park can once again be a vital part of the community's focus and pride, instead of a blight. And the same is true for AWSS.* Having come to that conclusion, Ben took out the reports and his tablet and started adding to his notes that he had begun to compile earlier that morning.

Before he knew it, Ben had been at the park for two hours, grateful that the unseasonably warm weather had accommodated his visit. It was time to head back to Connecticut, but before he did, Ben had an idea. He went to his car to retrieve the tool box he carried in his trunk, not sure his idea would work. Then he went over to the Holiday Park sign and found a way to take it down. Two people passing by watched what he was doing but said nothing, as Ben carried the sign to his car and put it on the back seat. Then he started for home, but decided to make one more stop.

When he watched the video with Charlie Mitchell during his visitor's session the night before, he noticed the name of the facility on the wall behind Charlie's television. It was "Myers Court Assisted Living Center," and Ben assumed it was someplace in the area close to where he was. He put the name into his GPS, and found that the Center was located in Lodi, not far from Englewood. Ben requested directions and set off to visit old Charlie to see how he was doing. He thought, *Charlie probably has no interest in seeing me, but at least I can pay him a visit to let him know I've made some mistakes.* It was Charlie who had presented Ben and his sister with their trophy and a $25 check for their three-legged victory. Maybe it was time for Ben to say thank you to Charlie, not just for the memories, but for a lifetime of service to AWSS.

Using his GPS, Ben got to Myers Court in about 20 minutes, just as it was getting dark. The place didn't look half bad, until Ben got inside and was confronted with elderly people, many in wheelchairs, sitting in the lobby area. Some were staring at nothing in particular; others had visitors sitting with them. There was a large Christmas tree in the lobby, and some of the staff nurses wore Santa hats as they walked through the lobby toward their appointed duties. There was an unpleasant aroma in the air, including some air freshener that was unable to hide the odor.

Ben went up to the reception area and asked, "Is there a resident here named Charlie Mitchell? I'm an old friend of the family." The receptionist checked her screen and said, "Yes, Mr. Mitchell is in 108C. You can go through this door and then use this security code to get through the locked doors." Before she would give him the code, however, Ben had to show the reception-ist his driver's license and sign in. "I'll keep your license here until you leave," she informed Ben, who proceeded through the first of three security doors.

As he got through the second door, he heard someone yell, "What the hell are you doing here?" When Ben turned to face the voice, it was a woman whom Ben did not know or recognize. "You have a lot of nerve showing your face," she said. "You don't know who I am, do you?" she asked, voice trembling with anger.

"I'm sorry, I don't," Ben replied, visibly shaken.

"I'm Victoria Rasmin, but you would have met me as Victoria Mitchell," she informed Ben. "I'm Charlie Mitchell's daughter."

Ben was surprised and a bit taken aback. He could feel his face blush as he stared at the woman, who was turning her own shade of red. Ben tried to explain why he was there, "I, yes, I was in the area and I, um, I thought," but before he could get very far, the woman interrupted him.

"You probably want to see what you can take from my father's room, you leech," Victoria sputtered. "You took just about everything else from him."

Ben had no response. "Yes, I was hoping to see Charlie to . . ." he began, but again Victoria interrupted.

"My father served you Holiday people for a long time and this is the thanks he gets," Victoria continued as she held out her hand, pointing across the hall. "You broke his heart, and now he will spend the rest of his days in this hole because of the financial setback that you provided when you let him go. You ought to be ashamed! No severance pay, no going away party, nothing. You, you," but before she could finish, a nurse in a Santa's hat passed by and said, "Please, keep your voices down."

Ben fumbled for an explanation, "Times were bad for the company. I did what I had to do to keep us afloat."

"Yes, you floated, while my father drowned. I don't know what you're up to coming here, but I think it best if you leave, *now!*" Victoria demanded. "Now! My father probably wouldn't even recognize who you are, so just leave."

Ben was totally embarrassed and flustered at that point, and said, "Yes, of course, I don't want to upset anyone," and made a bee line for the side door, heading out into the early evening darkness. He had to walk around the building to get back to the front, and he walked as fast as he could.

As Ben got in his car, he drove back toward the George Washington Bridge. As he drove over the Bridge, Ben shouted, "Oh crap! I left my driver's license at Myers Court!" But he was not about to go back. He had to get home, for he had a third visit ahead of him, and he wanted to be there for it. This weekend had turned out nothing like he expected, and he had a feeling that the third visitor would in some ways be the toughest one of all.

⠿⠿⠿⠿⠿⠿⠿⠿⠿

Ben got home around 7:30 PM, and having given no thought to dinner, he hadn't eaten anything since his hamburger on the way to Holiday Park. He scrounged around his kitchen and settled on some chips and salsa with a glass of juice for dinner. While he ate, Ben continued to read the consultant's report, which he still had not read front to back, instead picking around it, starting at different places and ending when he could no longer stomach what he read. All the while, Ben kept taking notes on his tablet, and had about 15 pages filled so far. The report said,

> *Ben's leadership style reflects his role as a communicator. Ben's ability to communicate effectively to his staff and employees is noted by its absence. Ben is simply not a good communicator. He spends little time engaging his leadership team, individually or as a group, in conversations about the future of AWSS and in what new strategic direction they should go to give AWSS its best chance of being successful in the future. For Ben, knowledge is power and he keeps most of that knowledge to himself.*
>
> *Because he does not practice inclusion in the manner in which he leads, he sees no need to communicate in the way described above. He seems unaware of, or perhaps doesn't care about, whether or not his leadership team and other employees are "in the loop" when it comes to business matters. This creates a sense of alienation from Ben which lends itself to a lack of motivation to go above and beyond what is required of them in terms of their daily work. Ben*

*is not a listener and he seldom seeks nor values the input of his leadership team as he makes decisions that affect the success of AWSS.*

*What he communicates to them usually are the decisions he has already made. Typically, Ben dismisses their ideas on initiatives ASWSS could pursue to remain profitable and lets them know that it is "his way or the highway" in terms of carrying out what he wants them to do, business-wise.*

Ben was trying to forget his visit to Myers Court, but it was heavy on his mind. *I did what I had to do*, he kept telling himself. *She doesn't understand. Costs had to be cut. Tough decisions had to be made*, Ben reasoned with himself. *The family can't blame me for where Charlie is. He should have managed his money better so he could've been in a better place.* Ben sounded like a defendant on the witness stand, and even he was beginning to doubt his own testimony.

Time seemed to move at a snail's pace as Ben ate and then went to his favorite couch to watch some TV. It was 9:30 PM, then 10, then 11:30 PM as Ben watched some hockey and then the movie *Elf*. Ben got up to check all his cable and DVD connections. Last night, he had unplugged them, but tonight he wanted to make sure everything was in working order. He wasn't sure what or who was ahead in the night hours as he prepared for his final visitor.

But that visitor once again delayed beyond Ben's ability to stand watch. At some point, Ben fell asleep, only to be awakened at about 1 AM by his door bell ringing. Ben jumped off the couch, rubbed his eyes, and thought, *Oh great. Now the visitors are ringing the doorbell, like a repairman.* He jumped up to the door and looked through the peephole, only to exclaim, "Oh my God!"

when he saw who it was. He turned around and pressed his back to the door, eyes wide in shock and confusion.

He threw open the door, only to hear a voice say, "Hello, Ben. Good to see you. May I come in?" The voice and the visitor belonged to Ben's sister, Miriam, who had passed away from breast cancer 12 years earlier. Ben was speechless, but as she entered, Miriam said, "We have a lot to talk about tonight, so let's get started right away."

⁕⁕⁕⁕⁕⁕⁕⁕⁕⁕⁕

"Miriam, I, you, how, I don't know what to say," the shocked Ben said, with eyes wide and mouth open.

"Well, you can say, 'Come in' to start," Miriam said, as she didn't wait for the invitation and walked right in. "You haven't done a thing to this place since the last time I was here," she said, hanging up her coat while taking a quick look around. "But I'm not here to decorate your home; we have a company to save." Miriam sat down and opened her briefcase. "Let's get to work," Miriam said in a matter-of-fact tone.

"Do you want something to drink?" Ben asked, still at a loss for words.

"Uh, no," Miriam said laughing and smiling. "I don't drink any more. It would go right through me!"

Ben thought he understood what she meant but didn't have the nerve to pursue it any further. Then he thought, *Well, the same can't be true for those other beer-guzzling consultants!*

"So you are the Spirit of Leadership Future?" Ben asked, but Miriam didn't say anything, just letting the question and answer register firmly into Ben's mind.

"Miriam," Ben said, "before we start, I have to tell you that I went over to Englewood today." Ben looked at Miriam, but she said nothing. "It was quite sad to see the park. It looked like a junkyard. Then I tried to go over and see Charlie Mitchell," and Miriam interrupted.

"I don't suppose he was too happy to see you," was Miriam's only response. "How's my son Jimmy doing?" changing the subject.

Ben looked down, avoiding Miriam's gaze, "Not good. He's pretty upset with me right now. In fact, it seems that everyone's pretty upset with me."

"And up to this point, it didn't seem to bother you, Ben," Miriam added. "What's happened to you?"

"What do you mean, 'What's happened to me?'", Ben responded with surprise and hurt in his voice. "I did what . . ."

Again, Miriam interrupted, "You did what you had to do. That's what you've told yourself and everyone else. But you didn't do what *you had* to do, you did what you knew to do, and the problem is that you didn't know very much."

Ben took a deep breath to respond, but decided against it.

"When you cut yourself off from your team, when you made the bottom line the main thing, the *only* thing, you lost your bearings, and have been lost ever since," Miriam said in a matter-of-fact manner. "Did you read the report?"

"I've been working my way through it," Ben said sheepishly.

"So that's a no I presume?" Miriam pressed Ben for an answer.

"Not all of it," Ben said, once again looking away.

"Okay, I'm here to show you the future, so let's get right to it," Miriam moved on, satisfied that Ben was at least being honest.

They both turned their attention to the screen, and saw the entrance to Ben's office building in New York City. Everything looked normal. The scene went over to the directory of companies present in the building and slowly scanned the list.

"Wait a minute," Ben said. "Where's AWSS? It's not on the list, and it should be close to the top."

As if someone had heard Ben, the view went back to the top and focused on the companies that began with the letter A. Ben was correct; AWSS wasn't there. "Where are we?" Ben asked Miriam, but she said nothing.

Then the camera scanned down to the tenants whose names began with M and Ben saw a name he didn't recognize, a name that was new to the list. "I never heard of Morris Security Services," Ben said to himself. "Who is Morris Services, and what are they doing on the eighth floor, which is where we are now?"

Again, Miriam said nothing. "Morris," Ben continued to process what he saw, "would that be Tommy Morris?" Miriam remained silent. "Tommy Morris took over AWSS and changed its name?" Ben asked, concluding that he was correct. "Tommy Morris took over AWSS and changed its name, that lowdown, ungrateful," Ben was at a loss for words, or rather the words he wanted to use were not appropriate in his sister's presence.

"Yes, Tommy came in and bought AWSS and its assets for a song when things bottomed out," Miriam said. "AWSS is no more!"

Before Ben could say anything else, the scene shifted to the eighth floor conference room, where Tommy was seated at the head of the table. Also present were Jimmy, Cheryl, and Jeff, engaged in a discussion, with the white board full of diagrams and charts. Then Ben spied something next to the white board, and shouted, "Hey, what's that next to the white board?" As if under his control, the scene focused on the portrait of Ben's great-grandfather, the same portrait that Ben had removed to make more room on the walls. "The guy takes over the company, changes the name, and wants to use our picture," Ben said incredulously.

"You don't get it, Ben," Miriam said softly, shaking her head. "Tommy had to change the name of the company, but at the same time, Tommy went back to the original vision statement of Great-Grandfather Fred in order to save the company—the same vision statement that you ignored and trampled in your quest to make money."

Miriam allowed those words to sink in. "Do you see my Jimmy sitting next to Tommy?" Miriam asked, knowing full well that Ben did indeed see him. "He was promoted to director of communications and operations, and he has done quite a good job. I am, or should I say, I will be proud of him. I always get confused when I see the future, but talk about it in the present," Miriam said, laughing at the irony. She laughed alone, however, for the irony was lost on Ben at the moment.

"Tommy Morris is running AWSS," Ben shook his head.

"Miriam," Ben asked, "is this the future the way it is, or the way it could be? Is it too late? Can this be turned around?" Just then, Ben noticed someone else. "Wait! Who is that sitting at the table?"

The camera, on Ben's cue, focused on a woman who Ben recognized. "I know that woman. Who is she?"

Miriam answered, "I think you met her today at the home when you went to visit Charlie. That's Charlie's daughter, who refused to allow you to see him." Again, Miriam fell silent as Ben processed it all. Then she continued, "Tommy reached out to the family and found out that the daughter was a single mom and out of work, so Tommy hired her as a way of saying thank you for all the years Charlie served AWSS. She is doing quite a good job."

Then Ben asked one more question. "They look like they all have the same document or report that they are reading and discussing. What is it?" but Ben felt he already knew.

"Why, it's the report that you are holding in your hand," Miriam responded. Then Ben saw one more person at the table, whose back had been to the camera. It was Francis, whom Ben had summarily dismissed.

"But now answer my question," Ben said, looking Miriam in the eye. "Is this reversible? Can this scenario be changed?"

Miriam nodded and said, "It can, but you don't have much time. It will start with reading the report and taking the steps that Francis recommended. What AWSS needs now are L.E.A.D.E.R.S., people who will apply the concepts found in that acronym."

"You will also need to rely on the team you currently have," Miriam continued. "That means you're going to have to get over the fact that you don't know it all, don't know most of it, but together you'll find some answers that hopefully will turn things around."

"What do you mean, *hopefully?*" Ben asked cautiously.

"There are no guarantees in business, Ben," Miriam responded. "You lost your way, and the company lost its way, but your only chance to recover is to become the L.E.A.D.E.R. you need to be. If you can recapture the spirit of Great-Grandfather Fred, you have a chance. But, there are no sure things in your case."

"Miriam," Ben began, "how did you get here? Where are you living right now? How do you keep up with all that's going on at AWSS?" Before he could continue, Miriam raised her hand and said, "Ben, you don't want to know all that. But I will say this. We all stay connected to the business through your memory and the memories of the customers and through the company's vision and reputation. But for the rest, you'll have to wait to find out."

Having said that, Miriam got up to leave. Ben looked at the clock and realized she had been there almost two hours, but it had seemed like only minutes. As she opened the door, Ben could not resist one more question, "Will you be back? Will I see you again?"

Miriam responded, "You'll see me again, but I can't say if I'll be back. That will be up to you." But before Ben could ask her to clarify what she meant, Miriam was out the door and vanished in the early morning cold.

Ben closed the door and said to himself, "Thank God this weekend is over!" but knew it was not over, for he found Francis' report and sat down on the couch, determined to read it through before he went to bed for a few hours of sleep.

# FINALE

Ben had set his alarm for 6:15 AM, his usual wake up time, even though he did not get to bed until 4:30. He usually caught the 7:15 AM train to New York. Although there would only be a skeleton crew at headquarters, he wanted to make an appearance. He was hoping Jimmy would be there, but wasn't sure if he was scheduled to be in.

Ben had his usual bagel, juice, and coffee, then packed his briefcase to head into town. He had the two reports, along with a tablet full of notes that he had jotted down earlier that morning. He had not only recorded as best he could remember what each consultant had said, he had also made notes and jotted down questions that he had as he read through the L.E.A.D.E.R.S. report.

When Ben got to Grand Central Station, he decided to walk to his office, which was a pretty good hike. He wanted both to energize himself because he had so little sleep and also to give himself more time to prepare for what he had to do. When he arrived, there was no receptionist and some of the lights were off. To his relief, Jimmy was already there, dressed in casual clothes. Ben stuck his head into Jimmy's office and said, "Good morning. Can I see you for a moment?"

Without saying anything, Jimmy followed Ben into his office. "Sit down, please," Ben said, "will you be here for a while today?"

"No," Jimmy replied, "Vivian and I and the kids are all going upstate to see her family. What are you doing in here today?"

"Jimmy," Ben began, "I want you to know I did a lot of thinking over the weekend. We don't have to go into it all now, but I want you to know that I stayed up most of last night, and I read the report. I need you to do a couple of things for me."

Jimmy sat stunned for a moment. "You read the report? All of it?" Jimmy asked in shocked disbelief.

"Yes, all of it," his uncle said. "Some of it doesn't make sense, but I think it will in time. Here's what I need you to do."

Jimmy was incredulous. *There was no way that his uncle was going to read it, he assumed, and there was no way he was going to implement it.* Something was up.

"I'm confused," Jimmy said. "You don't look well. Are you okay? I don't get it."

"Look, I said we would get into it after I have time to process it all myself," Ben said with a tinge of impatience, "but do this for me. Get in touch with Francis and see if he's willing to come back. If he is, schedule him to come back as soon as possible after the first of the year."

"Whoa," Jimmy said, "what else?"

"Then I want you to take some time over the holiday to think about the way forward with this domestic spying issue," Ben continued. "We need to revisit that and see if it was really worth all the fuss that it created for us. If not, then how can we get out?"

Jimmy said nothing, but now he knew that something radical had happened to his uncle. *Did he have a stroke?* he wondered. He had heard that some people's brains and consequently their behavior start to change before they have health issues like a blood clot or circulation problems.

"Finally, I need you to help me do something in the conference room, and then I'll let you go do your work before you head upstate."

With that, Ben led Jimmy to an office at the end of their suite that was used for storage, which had all kinds of old computers and desks. "What are we looking for?" Jimmy asked.

"I want to find the picture of my great-grandfather Fred, our founder. When we find it, I want you to help me put it back up in the conference room. It's time that I became the L.E.A.D.E.R. that he once was."

And with that, Jimmy was convinced that his uncle had lost his mind, just in time for Christmas.

Despite his uncertainty about what was happening, Jimmy began rummaging through the room. It only took a couple minutes before he found the picture in the corner behind an old beat-up desk with a computer monitor on it. "Here it is," he exclaimed, happy to have spotted it first. Jimmy held it up for Ben to see. The picture was dusty but none the worse for wear. Ben stared at it for a couple of seconds and then said, "Wonderful, I'm glad no one threw it away. It still looks pretty good."

Jimmy handed the picture to Ben and they walked down the hall towards the conference room. On the way there, Jimmy stopped at a custodian's closet and picked up a cloth and a bottle of cleaner.

When they entered the conference room, Ben walked over to the spot on the wall where the picture had been before he took it down, right next to the white board. They dusted off the picture and hung it there, making sure it was secure and level.

"There, I think great-grandfather would be pleased," Ben said with a slight sigh. Jimmy chimed in, "You sound like as if you knew him."

"Well, in a sense I feel like I've met him, I mean through the company that he built," Ben quickly explained, knowing that Jimmy would never understand what had happened to him over the weekend. "For now, Jimmy, why don't you go home and have a great trip with your family to Vivian's folks. Have a Merry Christmas and enjoy the time off. I'll see you after New Year's."

Jimmy said thanks and began walking out of the conference room, still not sure what to think of his uncle. "Are you leaving now?" he asked somewhat sheepishly. "In a bit," Ben replied. "I'm going to hang around here for a little while."

"Ok, you have a great holiday too," said Jimmy as he left the room. *I wonder what he's doing for Christmas?* he thought, as he headed for his office to close up for the day. *Oh well, who knows what he's going to do after the way he acted today.*

Ben sat at the conference table and just stared at Great-Grandfather Fred's picture. After a short while, he came out of his trance with a start as his head jerked back a bit. He realized he'd been in deep thought about his great-grandfather. *I wonder what kind of person he really was? What kind of leader was he? What was it actually like to work with him? What kind of place was AWSS when Fred and his son led the business?* All these thoughts and others swirled in his head while at the same time he contemplated the future of AWSS.

*I've got a lot of work to do if I'm to recapture what they created at AWSS. If I'm to develop the L.E.A.D.E.R.S. Model in me, like the report said, I need help. I'm not even sure where to begin.*

*What about getting a coach to help me? Ben thought. I've heard about CEOs hiring a coach to help them improve as a leader. Why not ask Francis to be my coach? He knows the L.E.A.D.E.R.S. Model and he could work with me and help me understand what it really means. He could do it with me one-on-one and still meet with the leadership team and others here at AWSS from time to time. I need someone from outside of AWSS to give me support and mentoring.*

Ben slapped both hands on the table and stood up, saying out loud to no one in particular, "Yes, that's what I'm going to do!" wondering if Jimmy had heard him. *I'll call Francis and see if he'll agree to help me figure out how to be the leader that AWSS needs right now. Wait. Why wait till next week. I think I'll call him now!* he said to himself.

Francis was surprised, stunned was more like it, to receive Ben's call. but they set a time in mid-January to reconnect. Both thought it would be best to get together at an off-site location, at least for the first time. After much discussion and times when Francis wondered why Ben had called or if this arrangement would work, Francis agreed to be Ben's executive coach. They agreed to use the consultant's reports as the guide for their relationship together, and talked through what the end product would look like as Francis worked with Ben.

While they paid attention to all the report, they especially worked on the SIC framework, for Ben needed a lot of help understanding how service, inclusion, and communication would enhance each one of the L.E.A.D.E.R.S. components. Francis assigned Ben reading to do, and they met one a month in person, and talked two times every week by phone.

Francis also told Ben that this kind of change in him would be challenging and take time, advising Ben that he needed to be patient and persistent. He encouraged Ben to seek feedback from his peers regarding his progress, to put his ego aside, listen to them, and keep an open mind. They talked about Ben practicing specific behaviors that reflect the L.E.A.D.E.R.S. Model so he could begin to experience what it's like to lead with those characteristics and for others to see the changes in action. Finally, Francis stressed the importance of Ben thinking about and reflecting on what was happening to him each week.

Through the weeks, Ben shared his successes, shortcomings, and perspective on his change journey. They discussed how others were reacting to Ben and the feedback he was getting from some of his peers. Francis listened, encouraged, and mentored Ben, sharing insights and offering suggestions to him about how he could get better as a leader and a person. Francis pushed Ben to reflect on his experiences and to think about how he felt about them.

They laughed a lot at some of Ben's stories, and Francis commiserated with Ben when he struggled with figuring out how to become the leader he wanted and needed to be. After they worked together for three months, Francis suggested that he periodically shadow Ben at work to observe firsthand how he was doing and to witness the reactions of his co-workers. Those experiences became good fodder for their coaching sessions.

All the while he was meeting with Francis, Ben met with members of the leadership team, usually once a month, to discuss the consultant's report and the L.E.A.D.E.R.S. Model. Several times, he met with other employees to do the same and made sure the information was shared with all the employees at AWSS. Ben worked hard to serve their needs, becoming a better listener and using his power to empower them to succeed.

It did not come naturally, but Ben worked to include others in his decisions and deliberations. And everyone was amazed when Ben began suggesting things to post on the company's Facebook page.

By the time summer came around, Ben had made some great progress at becoming the leader that AWSS needed. He wasn't there yet, but he sure was a good way along in the journey. Ben's perseverance, patience, and positive attitude remained in place as he continued to make changes to his behavior, his attitude, and how he viewed his role at AWSS, despite experiencing some missteps along the way.

Before they knew it, September was approaching. Ben asked Francis to visit AWSS before Labor Day and participate in a meeting with the leadership team that Ben planned to convene. Now that day had arrived.

Ben was seated in the AWSS conference room, waiting for the rest of the team to come in. He was facing the portrait of his great-grandfather that he and Jimmy had put up nine months earlier. It was now the Friday before Labor Day, and much had happened since that fateful Christmas weekend of Ben's family reunion at his Connecticut condo, which he no longer owned. He had sold it and moved back to New Jersey to be closer to the rest of the family and their legacy.

"Good morning," Ben said, as Francis walked in, "what time do you head out today?"

"I have a 2 PM out of LaGuardia that will put me home around 4:30," Francis replied. "We should easily wrap up this session well before noon. Maybe I can get an earlier flight."

"What are we going to cover today?" Ben asked, as the rest of the team entered the room. "You think we can complete the overview report?"

"Shouldn't be a problem," Francis responded.

Once everyone was in the board room, Ben spoke up. "Before we get started today, I want to make a few comments about where we have been the last nine months." Everyone got quiet and all eyes were fixed on Ben.

"First, I want to thank Francis for his input and work with us over these months as we have endeavored to embrace the concepts found in his L.E.A.D.E.R.S. program. I for one have benefitted greatly, perhaps the most, from this way of approaching leadership."

Ben continued, "I wanted to give you an update on the stock situation. Once we divested ourselves of any involvement in the domestic eavesdropping work, our stock went up a little, as you know. We have now bought back all the shares and we are once again a privately-held company." The room full of employees offered applause to signal their approval of the progress.

"One more thing, and this is by no means a command performance, but I would like to invite any and all of you to the dedication of the Charlie Mitchell pavilion at the newly renovated Holiday Park over in Englewood this Monday, Labor Day, at 1 PM," Ben added. "It won't be a long program, but all of Charlie's family will be there."

Cheryl spoke up and asked, "How did all that come about, Ben?"

"After I tried to visit Charlie last Christmas, I learned of how upset his family was and, quite frankly, I didn't blame them. I made a terrible mistake in handling Charlie's dismissal, and it caused a lot of pain and suffering," Ben said, looking out the window as he responded. "It took us more than a few meetings with me visiting the family members and Charlie's wife to apologize."

Ben was now looking back at the team. "We helped move Charlie to a much better care facility and get some improved medical treatment. We also brought in Charlie's grandson to oversee our corporate security division, which is based now back in Englewood. He's doing a good job, and he's paving the way for us moving our headquarters back there sometime next year."

Jeff chimed in, "I think your father would have been quite pleased with all you have done over these past months, Ben."

"Well, thank you, Jeff, I appreciate that. We have a long way to go to apply these principles we've been learning, or perhaps I should say I have a long way to go." Ben motioned to the picture of his great-grandfather and said, "I agree that old Grandpa Fred would be pleased, as we've made an effort to recapture the vision he had for AWSS when he founded the company. I feel better now that he's back in this room, watching over us and our proceedings."

Nephew Jimmy asked, "Will he be making the trip back to Jersey with us?"

"Oh yes," Ben said emphatically. "Wherever we go, I'll make sure that his presence goes with us."

Then Ben changed the subject, "Francis, perhaps as we get started today, you could once again go over the acronym L.E.A.D.E.R.S. and what each letter stands for. Then I would like to go over what we've done since January to apply what we've learned."

### L stands for leadership

- Leadership is based on relationship.
- Leadership creates opportunities for change and transformation in the lives of the parties involved.
- Leadership focuses on building meaningful teams.

### E stands for ethics

- Ethics is about more than finances and process; it's about the treatment of people.
- Ethics stems from character and virtue.

- Standards and values must be lived, not just discussed.

### A stands for alignment

- When people clearly understand the vision, mission and strategy of the organization, there is alignment.
- When employees understand how their job contributes to the fulfillment of the vision and mission, there is alignment.
- When employees' personal values are in agreement with the organization's values, there is alignment.

### D stands for decision making

- Leaders must humble themselves and acknowledge that they may not be the smartest one on the team, or the one with the best perspective on every issue at all times.
- Leaders take time to identify, gather and analyze the necessary information that pertains to any decision.
- Leaders work toward consensus by having the right people at the table, listening to their views, and factoring their input into the final decision.

### E stands for engagement

- Leaders do not motivate, but they create an environment where people are motivated (and not demotivated) to do their best work.
- Money is not the only motivator, and sometimes not the main motivator for people to produce excellence, especially for long term performance.
- Leaders must assume that not everyone is motivated by the same factors that motivate them. Rather, they get to know each team member to understand what motivates him or her.

### R stands for resilience

- Effective leaders meet inevitable obstacles and

setbacks with optimism and energy.

- Leaders employ emotional intelligence to help develop resilience in others.
- Leaders do not treat most failures as ultimate or terminal, but as learning experiences from which all can gain new insights to be applied in the future.

### S stands for stewardship

- Leaders understand they have a responsibility to leave a positive legacy for the leaders who follow them.
- Leaders have the attitude that the organization for which they work, along with its vision and mission, are entrusted to them as a loan. Thus they act as stewards and not owners, seeking to leave the organization and the world around it in a better place than when they first received it.
- Stewardship involves more than the financials, and includes a charge and responsibility to care for people, the greater community in which the organization functions, and the world at large.

As Francis led the review and ensuing discussion, it was Jimmy's turn to look out the window and reflect on the past nine months. To think that he had almost left AWSS to work for Tommy Morris, who had departed AWSS over the domestic spying project. Now that they were out of the spying business and the company returned to private ownership, Jimmy felt like he had a new lease on his work life. The fact that he was a part owner only made it better.

Jimmy would miss the view of the Manhattan skyline, but he would not miss the commute. The new offices were 15 minutes from his home, and he could even go home for lunch if he wanted to. Life was good, and the Holidays were back, as was AWSS.

At the Labor Day dedication, the weather was perfect and there were about 100 people present at the event. Ben played emcee and led a short program, explaining his family's presence that caused the park to be opened in 1933. He pledged support from the family and AWSS to maintain and improve the conditions and facilities in the park.

Then Ben made the big announcement. "It is with great pleasure that I announce today that AWSS is returning its corporate headquarters to Englewood, hopefully before the end of the year!" With that, there was applause from the crowd that included the mayor and city council. "Our Manhattan adventure is over, and our re-entry into Jersey is about to begin," Ben added.

Next to Ben was something that was covered in a dark sheet. "As we dedicate this pavilion today, the scene of so many happy childhood memories for me, we're also renaming the park." Having said that, Ben took off the sheet to unveil a new sign that read "Holiday Mitchell Park – Founded 1933 – Renamed September 2016." Charlie's family knew nothing of this and they looked pleased as Ben explained the change. The sign was to replace the one that Ben had removed during his visit the previous December.

"As we close today," Ben said, "I want to thank the Mitchell family and all the AWSS team for their cooperation in making today possible. We vow a close, working relationship with the city officials to keep this park relevant and useful. And we pledge ourselves to be the best LEADERS we can be as we once again take our place as a successful and valued corporate citizen of this great town."

With that, Ben concluded the dedication. He was

pleased that everyone seemed to be happy. It felt right to be back, and it felt good to be free of the burdens of the past that almost brought the company down. As things wound down and the people left the park, Ben stayed behind, sitting where he had sat nine months ago, reflecting on what had gone wrong and the changes that he had made. He thought of his three visitors and what they had shown him, and he could sense his own personal growth as he embraced the L.E.A.D.E.R.S. concepts. As Ben sat and thought, he was hoping that somehow his family who had gone on before him was also watching. He wondered if his great-grandfather and even his sister knew what had transpired not just today but over the past nine months.

Ben had no way of knowing for sure, but he was committed to see the process through so that no one would ever have to visit him again to remind him that it was the concept of L.E.A.D.E.R.S. that had made AWSS great over the years.

After an hour or so, feeling a sense of satisfaction and contentment, Ben walked home, for his new house was within walking distance of Holiday Mitchell Park.

# Consultant's Report

# CONSULTANT'S FEEDBACK REPORT FOR AWSS

## Prepared by Francis Johnson

### INTRODUCTION

In our years of leadership consulting and development, we at Miriam's Consultants and Coaches (MCC) have developed what we refer to as the L.E.A.D.E.R.S. Model of leadership. It is an acronym representing seven key leadership characteristics and practices that are essential for any person who is in a position of authority and leadership, whether in a corporation or nonprofit institution.

In this report, we will evaluate the leadership at Always Watching Security Systems (AWSS) and specifically, Mr. Ben Holiday. This introduction will serve to explain what each of the letters in L.E.A.D.E.R.S. Model represents, with three key aspects of each characteristic. We will then evaluate AWSS in each area on a scale of Excellent, Good, Fair and Poor. Following this introduction in our Consultant's Report, we will provide further explanation of each leadership trait. We provide an expanded description of what we found among AWSS' leadership along with some steps the company can take, in partnership with our consultants, to enhance every area of the L.E.A.D.E.R.S. Model.

Here is a brief explanation of the L.E.A.D.E.R.S.

Model along with the evaluation assigned to AWSS.

## L stands for leadership

1. Leadership is based on relationship.
2. Leadership creates opportunities for change and transformation in the lives of the parties involved.
3. Leadership focuses on building meaningful teams.

Effective leaders foster influential relationships among followers. Why? Because they realize that it not just about "the leader," but understand that it's about engaging in a process of leadership with followers, other leaders, customers and other stakeholders. The ultimate objective of relational leadership is positive change and transformation for both their organizations and the people with whom they work.

This type of relational, transformative leadership process is inclusive by nature. For an organization to function at its best, leaders must embrace and take advantage of the diversity of perspectives, attitudes, skills, and insights represented within an organization.

## AWSS Leadership Rating: POOR

## E stands for ethics

1. Ethics is about more than finances and process; it's about the treatment of people.
2. Ethics stems from character and virtue.
3. Standards and values must be lived, not just discussed.

Many organizations follow standard accounting procedures and pay their taxes on time. Yet they treat their people with disrespect or even disdain, ignoring their highest priority needs of growth, development, and involvement in meaningful work. What's more, leaders must realize that they are not an end unto themselves. They don't see or know it all, and therefore must be in constant dialogue with others to ensure that the leaders' perspective is not myopic, naïve or relative. Ethics is the linchpin for any successful leadership and will be undone by unethical behavior.

Leaders sustain and maintain ethical organizational behavior not just by seeking legal compliance among employees to a "set of ethical standards." More importantly, they build a culture that embeds into the organizational DNA, the ethical standards that are integral to the conduct of its business.

## AWSS Ethical Rating: POOR

## A stands for alignment

1. When people clearly understand the vision, mission and strategy of the organization, there is alignment.
2. When employees understand how their job contributes to the fulfillment of the vision and mission, there is alignment.
3. When employees' personal values are in agreement with the organization's values, there is alignment.

Fundamentally, the word alignment indicates that all are pulling in the same direction. Leaders align co-workers by making clear the direction in which the organization is heading and by gaining the commitment among them necessary to achieve its vision, mission, and strategy.

Strategic alignment is absolutely vital to the successful implementation of strategic change initiatives. The phrase "line of sight" is often used when speaking of this type of employee alignment with organizational strategy. This concept of line of sight refers to the ability of employees to not only knowing their organization's strategic goals but also what they need to do to achieve those goals.

Ensuring that there is alignment requires time and effort on the part of leadership. It means that leaders must regularly communicate the vision and mission in more than one way, repeating it so that people have a chance not just to hear, but to respond, ask questions, and obtain the clarity necessary for synergy of activity to occur.

AWSS Alignment Rating: FAIR

### D stands for decision making

1. Leaders must humble themselves and acknowledge that they may not be the smartest one on the team, or the one with the best perspective on every issue at all times.
2. Leaders take the time to identify, gather and then analyze the necessary information that pertains to any decision.
3. Leaders work toward consensus by having the right people at the table, listening to their views, and factoring their input into the final decision.

There is no more important practice in any organization than making good decisions. A good decision is first measured by the process used and not necessarily by the outcome. Often, unforeseen factors can enter into the equation after a decision is reached that impact the decision negatively. A good decision is one that is made when the right people spend the right amount of time with access to the right information. Then they take the time to explain the decision and its rationale to others who can then "buy in" and do all in their power to carry it out.

No matter what the nature of a decision may be, most often there will be those who disagree. They may even resist or try to sabotage the decision in some way. However, (and this is a big however) one thing leaders can always defend, regardless of the outcome, is the process that was used to arrive at the decision. If leaders have tried their best to follow the suggestions for making quality decisions discussed above, then they can argue with clarity that the process used was appropriate, rigorous and fair. This can go a long way toward convincing others that the decision was the best and right one to make.

AWSS Decision-Making Rating: POOR

### E stands for engagement

1. Leaders do not motivate, but they create an environment where people are motivated (and not demotivated) to do their best work.
2. Money is not the only motivator, and sometimes not the main motivator for people to produce excellence, especially for long term performance.
3. Leaders must assume that not everyone is motivated by the same factors that motivate them. Rather, they get to know each team member to understand what motivates him or her.

Peter Drucker once said, "Management's job is to find out what they are doing that keeps people from doing their best work and stop doing it."

In the transformational leadership model, there is a concept called individualized consideration. That includes the practice of challenging people to think outside the box and to empower them with the freedom to take on a task and do it in a way they feel is best. During this process, the leader shows empathy and support and maintains regular communication. Leaders are not afraid to celebrate the successes of their followers and give credit where credit is due. When leaders do these things, then their followers are engaged: contributing their creativity and energy without reservation, managing themselves rather than waiting on someone else to manage or direct their work.

Most studies show that money is not a good motivator where work is concerned, particularly in the long run. In fact, in many cases, money can hinder creativity and commitment. An effective leader works to understand what motivates each employee, and then strives to create a work environment where people are given roles and responsibilities that allow them to regularly perform according to their strengths and interests.

AWSS Engagement Rating: FAIR

### R stands for resilience

1. Effective leaders meet inevitable obstacles and setbacks with optimism and energy.
2. Leaders employ emotional intelligence to help develop resilience in others.
3. Leaders do not treat most failures as ultimate or terminal, but as learning experiences from which all can gain new insights to be applied in the future.

Resilience is that hard-to-define human characteristic that gives people the ability to withstand and respond to the challenges of life. Such resilience allows them to rebound from difficult circumstances and emerge ready to move forward with even greater resolve.

Today, resilience is considered an important individual as well as organizational trait, and is especially relevant given the often chaotic and uncertain landscape in today's corporate world. Resilience is one of the qualities of a "positive" organizational environment in which employees are much better suited to deal with the incredible pace of change they face while continuing to work towards the fulfillment of their company's vision and mission. It is this "bend but not break" attitude and behavior that enables employees to remain positive and productive while under the stress of ensuring organizational success.

An encouraging aspect of resilience is that this capacity can be understood and developed regardless of one's background or position within an organization. Those in leadership roles have a particular responsibility in this case to create work environments that support the growth of resilience among co-workers. Leaders must model the behaviors of resilience, such as being positive and optimistic, fostering a climate of mutual support, and seeing failure (in themselves or others) as a learning experience. Leaders who encourage the growth of resilience make their organizations intrinsically motivating places to work especially during times of challenge and change.

AWSS Resilience Rating: FAIR

### S stands for stewardship

1. Leaders understand they have a responsibility to leave a positive legacy for the leaders who follow them.
2. Leaders have the attitude that the organization for which they work, along with its vision and mission, are entrusted to them as a loan. Thus, they act as

stewards and not owners, seeking to leave the organization and the world around it in a better place than when they first received it.

3. Stewardship involves more than the financials, and includes a charge and responsibility to care for people, the greater community in which the organization functions, and the world at large.

Fundamentally, leaders as stewards are concerned about the health and happiness of their organization and the people who work there. Stewardship of financial assets are part of the leader's responsibility inasmuch as fiscal viability is necessary for the fulfillment of the organization's vision and mission. The pursuit of financial health, however, does not trump the welfare of people in the process. Leaders who get caught up in the race to make money at the expense of those who produce such profits are not stewards.

Leaders as stewards know their position is transitory in nature. They view the organization as on loan to them and that after they are gone the organization goes on. Thus, they commit themselves to make sure the organization is in better shape when they leave than when they assumed the responsibility of being its steward.

In addition, leaders as stewards know their organization does not exist in a vacuum. They are neighbors in a local community in which their business functions. As an individual would be expected to be a good neighbor, organizations are expected to do the same. This is not only an obligation; it also often makes good business sense. A healthy community contributes to the health of that organization's local operation, and the wise company invests in the health of the community as a means of enhancing its own health.

### AWSS Stewardship Rating: POOR

# SIC Practices

In addition to the seven components of the L.E.A.D.E.R.S Model, leaders must pay attention to three important disciplines that will improve their effectiveness where leadership, ethics, alignment, decision making, engagement, resilience, and stewardship are concerned. These three disciplines are serving, inclusion, and communication, what we refer to as SIC influencers. The SIC practices act like vitamins that make the L.E.A.D.E.R.S Model more vigorous and healthy. If leaders will focus on these three practices, they will automatically improve in every area represented in the L.E.A.D.E.R.S. Model.

## S – An attitude of service

Robert Greenleaf, father of the servant leadership movement, defined servant leaders as those who serve others' highest-priority needs. When an organization is infected with an attitude of service, it is practiced not just in relationships with customers, but between everyone in and outside the organization. Leaders serve followers, followers serve one another along with clients or customers, and the organization serves the community at large. Service will enhance any organization's ability to embody the concepts found in the L.E.A.D.E.R.S. Model.

## I – A commitment to inclusion

There is a saying that states, "All of us are smarter than one of us." That is why leaders look to involve as many people as possible in every area of the organization. They include them in the decision-making process so the organization can benefit from everyone's expertise and unique perspective. One key trait where inclusion is practiced is the art of listening and asking good questions. Leaders who ask and listen can gain a competitive advantage for their organization and take advantage of work synergies where people together can accomplish more than then they can as individuals.

## C – The ability to communicate

Organizational health and success are dependent on having an informed workforce. Obviously, that means that leaders must communicate effectively. Leaders who do so use a variety of methods and media to deliver messages that are honest and transparent. Communication occurs regularly across all levels of leadership and responsibility. They make sure that important news is distributed through both formal and informal networks. In addition, leaders value two-way communication, asking questions, listening empathetically, engaging in dialogue, and encouraging feedback that is genuine and honest.

This concludes the introduction to our report. We now turn our attention to a more in depth evaluation of AWSS and its leadership, using the L.E.A.D.E.R.S. Model as the standard. It is our hope that AWSS will seriously consider our findings, and allow MCC to assist them in developing the seven characteristics in the L.E.A.D.E.R.S. Model and apply the SIC practices throughout the organization.

## The Main Report

As explained in the Introduction, MCC advocates that the L.E.A.D.E.R.S. Model be followed in order that effective leadership may produce a healthy business environment in any organization. Having presented the framework for the Model in the Introduction, I will now expand on my findings and the way forward for Mr. Ben Holiday and the AWSS leadership team.

## Leadership

Conventional thinking often equates leadership with the person who has the title, someone who is identified as such by his or her position. If a person is the president, director, CEO, or manager, then that person is the "leader" and all others who are not in a "leadership" position are, by default, followers. Leadership in the L.E.A.D.E.R.S Model, however, is understood as something quite different.

According to the L.E.A.D.E.R.S Model, leadership is not about the position or power of the leader. Rather, leadership is a process that occurs when leaders and followers together engage to accomplish clearly-established purposes or goals. This process of leadership is possible because leaders and followers are in a relationship with one another based on influence. This influence relationship is *not* based on power or position, and is *not* the result of coercion, threats, intimidation, or manipulation. Rather, this influence relationship occurs through thoughtful persuasion, positive interpersonal connections, and the freedom to choose whether or not to be in such a relationship (Rost, 1993).

This view of leadership certainly turns conventional thinking on its head. Instead of leaders leading by "wielding their power and authority," leaders do the necessary and sometimes challenging work of leading by getting to know their followers, interacting with them regularly, discussing with them the nature of the organization's business, and, through encouragement and support, strengthening their commitment to its vision and mission.

This kind of leadership is not easy. It requires that leaders take on the herculean task of creating a work environment in which leadership as a process can take place. It means dealing with all sorts of different people, some who are not easily persuaded or motivated to engage in the process of leadership.

For leaders to lead in this way, there must be effective communication. Communication is a key to establishing the type of influence relationship with others that is described above. Such leaders view communication as a "conversation." This means that leaders communicate regularly with all employees, use a variety of formal and informal means, and ensure that whatever the message may be, everyone in the organization understands its true meaning. Leaders who communicate effectively engage others in open, honest, and accurate discussions of information that is important and necessary for organization success. They promote dialogue, expecting to receive helpful feedback and to use that feedback to inform future organizational development and direction.

First and foremost, leaders who are effective communicators practice "inclusion." They begin with the belief that *all* employees must know what is "going on," because they value employees as important assets in the success of the organization. Communicating regularly helps to avoid the vacuum of silence that is often filled with rumors and inaccurate information.

Second, leaders connect with employees not only using the "official" methods through memos, emails, video presentations, and formal meetings, but also by talking with them in the hallways, on the shop floor, and in their offices. Leaders understand the influence and power of the informal networks within their organization when it comes to communication, using them to help distribute important news and to obtain feedback.

Finally, effective communication occurs when the message has been received and is understood. To verify this is the case, leaders "listen." They do more than talk; they ask questions. They seek to find out how team members interpret what they are hearing. It makes little sense for leaders to deliver a message without knowing what employees really hear and understand. This kind of two-way communication helps to ensure that all parties "are on the same page" and, at the same time, builds confidence among employees that what they have to say matters.

When leaders communicate effectively, they generate trust among all employees. By reflecting a positive "ethos" or character through how and what they communicate, they express authenticity and model transparency, not only about themselves but also about the organization. As a result, they build the kind of influential relationships that are necessary to be effective leaders.

Ben's leadership at AWSS is best described as top-down and authoritative in nature. Leadership is based on power and position and not relational influence. Ben is not collaborative by nature, preferring to work alone, with little interest in establishing a positive relational dynamic with his managers or other employees. He cares little about the interests, professional aspirations, or personal affairs of his employees. He spends very little time, if any, getting to know those who work at AWSS. Ben's main concern regarding his employees is that they show up on time, perform their assigned work as prescribed by Ben, and not leave a minute early at the end of the work day. Ben assumed his role as president and CEO with the attitude that success at AWSS would be measured in terms of money and profit and that he was the only one in the organization capable of achieving that kind of success.

Ben's ability to communicate effectively to his staff and employees is defined by its absence. Ben is simply not a good communicator. He spends little time engaging his leadership team, individually or as a group, about the future of AWSS and in what new strategic direction they should go to give AWSS its best chance of being successful in the future. For Ben, knowledge is power and he keeps most of that knowledge to himself.

Because he does not practice inclusion in the manner in which he leads, he sees no need to communicate in the way described above. He seems unaware of, or perhaps doesn't care about, whether or not his leadership team and other employees are "in the loop" when it comes to business matters. This creates a sense of alienation from Ben, which lends itself to a lack of motivation to go above and beyond what is required of them in terms of their daily work. Ben is not a listener and he seldom seeks or values the input of his leadership team as he makes decisions that affect the success of AWSS.

One of the key elements in leadership, according to the L.E.A.D.E.R.S Model, is the ability to create effective teams, teams that contribute to the success of the organization. Ben's inability to see his leadership team as an important asset has really hurt AWSS as it attempts to navigate the current competitive environment. Consequently, initiating changes that would help keep AWSS profitable are unfortunately impossible at the very time it desperately needs such transformation.

When Ben made his decision to initiate the new domestic surveillance program, he did not communicate with or obtain input from his leadership team, let alone other employees, that he was considering such a move, nor did he seek their input. When he finally announced this decision, it came as a complete surprise to everyone at AWSS. This resulted in feelings of alienation, frustration, and mistrust towards Ben. This example indicates his lack of effectiveness as a communicator.

The real tragedy of Ben's leadership is that he inherited an organization in which effective, relational leadership was the standard practiced throughout AWSS. His father, grandfather, and great-grandfather created a company in which employees were valued as people, that became successful through great customer relationships, and whose purpose went beyond the business bottom line, recognizing its responsibility to the community and its citizens.

Ben needs to realize that his leadership style and all of the attitudes and behaviors that accompany it are not working. AWSS is not achieving the success, missionally and financially, that he thought would happen when he became its leader. For Ben to become the type of relational leader that was evident among his predecessors, he must take a long, hard look at himself as a person and as a leader. He needs to seriously consider the content of this report. He must take to heart all of the descriptions, conclusions, and recommendations that are included, through the lens of the L.E.A.D.E.R.S Model and begin the challenging task of becoming the leader that AWSS needs at this time. This will not be a "quick fix." Such change takes time. Ben and those at AWSS must be patient.

As Ben's leadership development journey takes

place, there will be starts and stops, bumps in the road, mistakes made, and progress achieved. Ben needs to remain open to reasonable and respectful feedback from his leadership team and employees as he travels though this new territory. The end is clear—Ben must become the leader necessary for AWSS to achieve its vision and mission. However, the trip is less certain. It's up to Ben and his co-workers to stay the course though these next months and perhaps years as Ben works out the changes that he must make to be the leader that would make his predecessors proud.

## Ethics

The first "E" in the L.E.A.D.E.R.S. Model refers to ethics and the ethical values and behavior of leaders and their organizations. This is a major problem in today's society and workplace and is foundational to successful leadership according the to the L.E.A.D.E.R.S. Model.

Frequently, when unethical behavior in the workplace is made public, it has to do with individuals who have engaged in some sort of financial misdeed. "Cooking the books," insider trading, stealing from the company, or price-fixing are just some of the misdeeds that make the news when unethical behavior is reported. We're amazed, shocked, and in disbelief when a "good" person is found out to have done some bad things in a "good" company. We usually attribute it to faulty strategy, or incorrect service or product design, but seldom look at the ethical underpinnings of the leadership team or corporate culture.

Unfortunately, what is often left out of these conversations in the workplace is the much more common occurrence of unethical behavior that involves the mistreatment of employees. Every day, in one organization after another, employees at all levels are exploited, manipulated, mishandled, and even bullied by supervisors, peers, and other co-workers. Poor leadership, especially when it pertains to the treatment of others, is unethical leadership. The L.E.A.D.E.R.S. Model focuses on that particular aspect of unethical behavior.

Ben Holiday has taken himself and AWSS down the slippery slope of unethical behavior. Ben has compromised the historic core values of AWSS, established at its founding by his great-grandfather and well established in the culture by the time Ben assumed the role of CEO. Those foundational principles included the notion that AWSS was like a family and all those who were employed there were considered to be the company's most valuable resource.

Qualities such as integrity, compassion, transparency, and most importantly, inclusion, were all practiced by Ben's predecessors. Employees as all levels were treated ethically and, as a result, their loyalty and commitment to the vision, mission, and success of AWSS were strong and resolute. They constantly communicated formally and informally with employees and were transparent about the company's financial status.

This type of ethical behavior was built upon the character and virtue of these leaders who preceded Ben. They were people who exuded integrity, courage, care, compassion, loyalty, respect, and kindness, among other traits. As a result, those who worked at AWSS knew that their leaders would treat them as valued partners and create environments in which they could thrive.  Ben lacks these virtues.

Because of Ben's lack of character in this respect, he cannot see the treatment of his leadership team and other employees as ethical issues. He can't imagine that there would be any principle or set of personal qualities guiding his behaviors other than the "bottom line." What only matters to Ben seems to be *his* view of what makes a company successful, and that means getting the job done his way. If someone isn't producing, he doesn't care why, he just wants it corrected immediately and according to his directive. If it means firing that person, then that's what he will do regardless of its effect on that individual. Consider what happened to Tommy Morris.

Tommy Morris was employed at AWSS as its Director of Business Development. He was an idea guy and often recommended innovative approaches to develop new market opportunities. Tommy was especially interested in exploring the ways social media and other cyberspace applications could be used as a means of marketing the services of AWSS. Tommy also criticized Ben's practice of top-down decision making and his lack of creating a collaborative, team atmosphere among his leaders. In particular, when Tommy found out about Ben's plan to expand the surveillance program initiative, he expressed his opposition to doing so, considering it a bad business, unethical, and another example of making a significant decision without consulting members of the leadership team.

Ben fired Tommy, no longer willing to tolerate his behavior, even though Tommy's ideas had great potential to increase AWSS market share. After being let go, Tommy moved on to another competitor and became very successful in that role. In fact, his new company has taken on additional business that either was or could have been provided by AWSS and has surpassed it in terms of annual revenue (based on its last annual report).

It is clear that Ben is unaware of this significant shortcoming of not seeing the ethical implications of his decisions and his treatment of AWSS employees. He needs to understand the effect that his unethical behavior has had on AWSS and its employees, and then make the decision to change his attitude and behaviors. Once he does this, there are several things he can do to develop the capacity to act ethically.

The first action Ben must take is to revisit the core values that his great-grandfather established when he started AWSS and that his successors took to heart. I introduce these values here, but I will discuss them more fully in the next section on alignment. They include:

- Develop the potential of all staff.
- Serve the communities where AWSS has a presence.
- Provide for a seamless leadership succession to ensure that the AWSS' traditions are maintained from generation to generation.
- Share company success with those who have a role in making it happen.
- Create a family atmosphere at work.
- Always communicate openly and with transparency.

Ben must understand how these values were deeply embedded in the culture of AWSS. He must realize that these values were not only "right" in principle, but understand why they worked—why AWSS became successful as a result of grounding its business on these values.

Next, Ben must own these cherished values for himself. They cannot just be "words on a poster" that are displayed on a wall. He must embody them. He has to begin the process of changing his perspective—what he considers to be ethical and unethical—which then can lead to a shift in his attitude and, hopefully, a change in his behavior.

As this happens, it's important that Ben

communicate to his leadership team and employees that it will no longer be "business as usual" at AWSS, that this perspective regarding his ethical view of things is changing, and explain why this is happening. Words or slogans alone, however, will not make a difference. It's essential that Ben begin modeling this changing ethical perspective through his behavior. And while Ben shows the way, he must also let those at AWSS know what these new ethical expectations apply to everyone.

Ben also needs to listen to others in his organization when it comes to establishing and maintaining ethical standards of behavior. In most cases, companies include individuals who represent a collection of beliefs and commitments regarding what is the "right and wrong" thing to do. As Ben develops his own ethical perspectives and begins to change how he sees things ethically, it will be helpful for him to consider what others at AWSS think. This process of listening to others will create "collective reasoning" among Ben, his leadership team, and other employees, leading to a greater buy-in to the establishing of ethical standards, attitudes, and behaviors that can more easily and consistently be implemented.

It will take a bit of time, but gradually Ben's leadership team and employees should move beyond the "what is with this guy?" skepticism and begin believing that Ben is for real, that he has changed and he expects them to follow his lead. As this transition takes place, the kind of "family" atmosphere at AWSS that was in place until Ben became CEO will be felt by both its employees and its customers. They will feel valued, they will feel respected, and they will know that AWSS is a place of integrity in how they are treated and how business decisions are made. The "bottom line" will be measured not only in terms of financial success, but also according to the level of satisfaction and meaning that employees receive from working at AWSS.

## Alignment

The letter A in the L.E.A.D.E.R.S. Model stands for alignment. Before days of front-wheel drive on most vehicles, it was possible for a car to be out of front-end alignment, which meant that the car would ride roughly, pull to one side or the other, and wear down tires un-evenly. It required an adjustment from a mechanic, and even then, hitting a rough bump in the road could cause the alignment to go out of kilter again.

When an organization is out of alignment, it pro-duces the same results as those older vehicles. The orga-nization's journey is subject to wear and tear along with a rough ride. Alignment begins at the top with senior management, for if the organization is not in alignment there, it certainly won't be in alignment any place else.

Alignment involves the leadership team being on the same page, so to speak, with one another. There is clarify of the organization's vision, mission, and strate-gy—where it is going and how it will get there. There is a clear understanding of the goals, and the strategies to achieve those goals. Alignment is not magic, but rather requires hard work, as the leadership team discusses and reaches agreement on the direction, but then allows people throughout the rest of the organization to take time to also be on the "same page."

This processing time is often overlooked by leaders, who spend large amounts of time debating and clarifying direction, vision, and goals, only then to make a 10-minute announcement to the rest of the organi-zation, who are then expected to be onboard with the decision instantly. The leaders should allow almost the same amount of time for the rest of the organization to come to grips with their decision as it took those leaders to reach that decision. There should be the same amount of debate, listening, questions and answers, and informal discussions so that the direction is clearly understood not just by leaders, but by everyone who has a stake in the decision made or direction established.

In the case of Ben Holiday and AWSS, there was clearly no alignment among the leadership team and the rest of the company. Ben made unilateral decisions, as best exemplified by his decision to pursue the domestic surveillance initiative. When the direction of the company was discovered by others on the team, they were predictably upset, wondering why they had not been included in the decision or had it explained to them, once the decision was made.

That tension led to the staff shake up, resulting in the dismissal of Tommy and others who Ben perceived were not in agreement with the direction he had selected. Ironically, it was actually a step toward alignment when Ben addressed the lack of unity on the part of his leadership team. Yet, the heavy handed way the transition was handled caused many who had relationships with Tommy and his team to experience anger and frustration at the direction the company was taking.

Tommy's departure was the fruit that came from Ben's departure from AWSS' core values. As determined by staff interviews and reviewing AWSS historical documents, the AWSS values were a commitment to:

**1. Develop the potential of all staff.** AWSS staff were encouraged to pursue college degrees and any other training that would contribute to their professional development. The company paid for the training, and each employee was expected to enroll in one workshop or seminar annually, with leadership approval, that would contribute to the area over which they had responsibility.

2. Serve the communities where AWSS has a presence. AWSS invested in the communities where they were based and where they had a significant presence. Their thinking was that their employees and their families often lived in those neighborhoods, and AWSS wanted to improve the quality of life for those families.

3. Provide for a seamless leadership succession to ensure that the AWSS traditions continue from generation to generation. Family businesses are only as effective as the leadership the family can provide for the company. AWSS was fortunate to have three generations of leaders that maintained the company's mission and values in the face of challenging business conditions.

4. Share company success with those who have a role in making it happen. AWSS has a reputation of paying their people well, but salary was not the only investment they made in their people. They were the first to hire women security officers, and the company paid childcare benefits. Their bonus plan was the envy of the industry, and they took good care of those who cared for AWSS.

5. Create a family atmosphere at work. Leadership took great pains not to think of their people as "only" security guards. They went out of their way to become acquainted with employee's families and sponsored corporate events that were family-friendly. It was not unusual for AWSS to help pay college tuition for employee's children and to assist when employees purchased their first home.

6. Communicate openly and with transparency. Before the term "management by walking around" was coined, AWSS leadership was doing it. It was not unusual for the CEO or other high-ranking official to show up

even during night shifts to talk and listen to the needs and concerns of their people. There was a monthly staff meeting that was open to all during which leadership would share company news and direction (the meetings were recorded, if you can believe it, using reel-to-reel technology to start so night-shift workers could listen on their own time).

Shortly after becoming CEO, Ben ceased to pay attention to the company's founding principles. That fact was best exemplified when Ben replaced his great-grandfather's picture in the conference room with a big-screen TV. Ben had forgotten the AWSS commitment to people, and had instead replaced that value with the pursuit of profit and growth. Ben stopped talking to his team and ignored the concept of inclusion as a motivating principle that helps align staff and customers with the company's values and purpose. Those actions created suspicion, rumors, and a culture of "silos" where everyone did their work isolated from others, seldom asking many questions or getting answers to the ones they had the courage to ask.

We assigned a "fair" rating for this particular practice even though we found employee alignment to have serious problems. There is still a remnant of "old timers" who remember the company as it was, and have tried to maintain a commitment to the core values. We liken their activity to what is called "guerilla tactics," where an operation exists under the radar, so to speak. There is still a core of committed employees who are doing business as AWSS has done in the past, in spite of the toxic environment created by Ben's alignment insensitivities.

Our recommendation is that Ben Holiday face the reality of the dysfunction in his operation and do what he must do to recapture the governing values of the AWSS founders. This is achievable, but will require a transformation on the part of Ben, which in turn must spill over into the company's frustrated and intimidated leadership team. There is also a concern that more jobs will be lost, which only causes people to dig deeper trenches to protect themselves from crossfire and attack.

The AWSS situation is critical, but there is still time to fix it, but only if Ben is willing to pursue the A in L.E.A.D.E.R.S., which is alignment. If Ben can work to have everyone, including himself, recommit to the core values and vision of a transformed AWSS, then we are confident that the momentum the company had can be recaptured and the rich history of this once-vibrant organization can be regained.

## Decision Making

In life and work contexts, leaders make decisions as part of their daily responsibilities. The quality and outcomes of those decisions determine the level of the leader's effectiveness. That is why the "D" in the L.E.A.D.E.R.S. Model stands for decision making.

The unfortunate and harsh reality, however, is that often the decisions leaders make are poor ones. In many cases, they don't quite understand what went wrong with those poor decisions. Therefore, it is difficult to improve the quality of future decisions until leaders understand what went wrong. Is it that things didn't go as expected, or does it have to do with how the decision was made—or both?

For these reasons, it is important that leaders improve their ability to make quality decisions. Leaders need to understand what contributes to making poor decisions and how to overcome those potential shortcomings. Is there really a process that leaders can follow to help them make better, faster, and more effective decisions? Are there problems with how leaders go about collecting any data, and how the data is analyzed that is used to inform decisions? What about the roles of leaders and followers in the decision-making process? All of these issues are significant and need to be examined for leaders to improve their decision-making skill.

To begin this discussion, it is important to consider the different categories of decisions that are made. Often referred to as "Type 1 and Type 2," these categories distinguish between the kinds of decisions that are daily, routine, and predictable (Type 1) and those that are novel, unusual, and much less predictable in their outcome (Type 2). Type 1 decisions abound in daily life and include everything from the way people get ready to go to work to processes and practices that are ordinary organizational standards.

Type 2 decisions address complex issues that require significant data collection, analysis, and evaluation before the best choice can be made. Making significant, strategic changes that have a major effect on the future of an organization are also Type 2 decisions. It is the Type 2 decisions, those that keep leaders up at night wondering what is the "right thing" to do, which ae the focus of this report.

In making Type 2 decisions, leaders often engage in the following process:

- The issue is identified for which a decision must be made.
- Data and information are gathered that help understand the nature of the issue or problem.
- This information is analyzed and used to determine what course of action should be taken.
- When the decision is made to take a

particular course of action (or not to take one), an announcement is made and the decision is implemented, believing that it is a good decision.

It sounds straightforward, rational, and simple, doesn't it? Leaders know from past experiences that making a decision is not a straightforward or simple process. Some have described the process of making decisions as "a flowing stream, filled with debris, meandering through the terrain of managers and their organizations" (McCall and Kaplan, p. 15). That description doesn't sound straightforward or simple. In fact, the context for making a decision is often complex.

In addition, leaders do not always act with complete rationality. Various factors affect their ability to think and act rationally, and these limitations affect their ability to make quality decisions. Many researchers have found, despite the perception that leaders are intelligent, rational beings, that the human brain has limitations that can affect a leader's capacity to make quality decisions.

Leaders may not accurately identify the real problem or issue with which they are dealing. As a result, they misinterpret what data should be collected, either collecting the wrong data or ignoring the correct information that merits their attention. Data that is collected may be misinterpreted, leading to a decision based on false assumptions or conclusions. What's more, the decision may not be effectively implemented, even if it was the correctly conceived.

Despite the inability to be fully rational beings and given the complexity of making decisions, it is possible for leaders to become better decision makers, thus improving their decision-making scorecard. To help achieve that goal, it's important to focus on the factors that can negatively influence the thought processes while considering any decision. Once they are aware of these factors, leaders can then understand how to enhance their performance as they analyze the circumstances surrounding any decision.

First, let's look at the issue of identifying the nature of the problem or issue for which a decision must be made. Leaders must make sure they have properly framed the issue; that is, they need to accurately understand what is "really going on" or the true cause of this issue that they face. If they do that, then they may end up attributing the wrong causes for the problem and consequently proceed to a decision that will have little or no bearing on solving the issue.

Second, leaders must seriously consider who should be involved in the decision-making process. Having the right people at the table, so to speak, will make a big difference when working through the process of determining the true nature of the problem or issue and then considering what course of action is best to take. Too often, leaders miss the mark when it comes to making certain they receive the best input possible by not including all of the relevant stakeholders during the decision-making process.

Third, it is important to know what data is necessary to create a full, accurate picture of the issue at hand and where to find such relevant information. Without a full range of appropriate material, the decision is more likely to be shortsighted or malnourished. That is why having multiple points of input from many people (what we again refer to as inclusion) is important to not only having the right data at hand but also to interpreting that data correctly.

Leaders should also strive to develop a process that creates a consensus among those directly involved in making a decision. In this case, consensus does not necessarily mean that everyone is in total agreement with the final decision. What is does mean is that during the process of debate, discussion, and analysis of the data relevant to the decision, all of those involved believe their perspectives have been given full consideration, even if the final decision is not one they would have recommended.

Those who disagree "stand down" after making their case, making a commitment to support the decision because the process included a fair opportunity to share and consider their concerns. This consensus process builds support and buy-in even though 100% of the participants may not be in total agreement.

As president and CEO of AWSS, Ben Holiday uses his position to make all decisions relative to business development, delivery of security services, finance, equipment purchases, employee policies, and employee hiring and firing. All managers and supervisors essentially do Ben's bidding, and have little if any influence in the way day-to-day operations are carried out. As a result, the creative potential of those who work at AWSS is stifled.

There is no emphasis on "team" or collaborative decision-making. Because of this, Ben's decisions are often short-sighted and are made without seeking the potential important insight that AWSS directors, managers, supervisors, and other employees could provide. Often shared from this group were statements such as, "I could have helped Ben with [that] decision, but he wouldn't listen to me." And, "Our group had data that could have avoided [the poor decision that got us into some trouble] if Ben would have been willing to consider what we knew. But he didn't and we lost a lot of money on that deal."

Ben's decision-making style and process reflect his phobia that causes him to stay in control of all aspects of AWSS and its business. For Ben, making decisions by himself with little or no input from others represent his leadership power. As far as Ben is concerned, holding on to this power by controlling the decision-making process is necessary for AWSS to be profitable. (Ben maintains the illusion that he alone is responsible for its success.)

For Ben to break this pattern of unilateral decision making, he must begin to see the shortcomings of his approach. One way he can see how his style of decision making is not working is to take an honest look at the financial performance of AWSS. Currently, AWSS is losing money. Yes, there are external factors that may be affecting business given the competitive and increasingly global nature of its business. Poor decisions made by Ben, however, are the primary cause at this point for AWSS to be bleeding red at the rate it is today.

Ben needs to take an honest look at the numbers and reconsider the decisions he made in the last several years that have contributed to this crisis. At some point in this examination process, he has to realize it was the decisions he made, all by himself, without the input of his very talented and creative leadership team, that have contributed to the slide in AWSS profitability. If the data can help him see this, then perhaps it will give him an incentive to become the type of relational, inclusive leader who will make quality, strategic decisions that are necessary to "right the ship" at AWSS.

## Engagement

The second E in the acronym L.E.A.D.E.R.S. stands for engagement. There is much being written and said about engagement in the 21st century, and for good reason. There has never been a greater need for an engaged workforce for the following reasons:

In most organizations, then, it is no longer a question of middle managers' allowing workers more choice and participation. Many levels of middle-management and supervisory positions have been eliminated, and an organization needs its workers to take on many of the rules. Workers are often in different locations from their managers, making close supervision impractical. Instead of complying with detailed rules, workers are now asked to be proactive problem solvers. They must make adjustments, coordinate with other organizational players, innovate, and initiate changes. Workers are becoming strategic partners of top management, deciding the actions needed at the grassroots level to meet their organization's goals (Thomas, 2000, pp. 9-10).

There are two key disciplines that will enhance engagement, and those are communication and inclusion. People want to know and be in the know, and they want to have a sense that they are contributing not just to the bottom line, but to the essence of the institution itself. They are looking for meaningful work where they can express their own meaning and values.

Money is less and less of a motivator for workers, especially where creativity and meaningful work are concerned. In fact, money can actually hinder work when it detracts from team-building and blurs the focus of the organization's highest priority tasks.

The issue of rewards has been debated and studied where work motivation is concerned. The concept of rewards such as pay, perks, awards and recognition are generally referred to as extrinsic motivators. Companies have pursued a course to discover the right mix of money, bonuses, and other rewards to get the desired results from employees.

It is our contention that *no one* works solely for money. As you read that statement, you may respond by asking, "Are you kidding? No one would work for free; everyone needs to get paid." While that's true, let us explain our rationale for coming to that unusual statement. As we do, we acknowledge the impact that Alfie Kohn's seminal work, *Punished by Rewards: The Trouble with Gold Stars, Incentive Plans, A's, Praise, and Other Bribes*, has had on our approach to engagement.

We would argue that almost no one works for money, but rather they work for what the money represents. Those who work take their salary and exchange it for goods and services. Those may include housing, food, vacations, retirement, college education, entertainment, and the like. If someone is working so they can take their annual trip to the Super Bowl for a vacation, then their motivation is that trip, not the money.

Someone else would hear of the Super Bowl plans and think, "I would never spend money on that. It's not important to me. I would rather buy a winter home down South." Therefore, that person is working for what the money can do to get them into their dream home. They convert their extrinsic reward—money and bonuses—to an intrinsic reward—the Super Bowl or a winter home.

Even the people who during the Depression years kept all their money in the mattress did not work for money. They worked for the feeling they got when they slept on top of their money. It gave them a sense of security that they could put their hands on their money without going to the bank, and the sense of safety in case the bank failed, causing them to lose their money.

What are the implications for employee engagement if our theory that no one works for money is correct? The implications are that leaders must discover what motivates their team members to work, and do all they can do to cooperate with those motivations. Leaders must understand that "one size does not fit everyone," for the motivations to work will be different for each person.

What's more, people regularly work for free when they volunteer their services to an organization with which they closely identify. There are a host of things that motivate people—a sense of order and organization, happy customers, adding up numbers that produce accurate reports, just to name a few—and if leadership can match those motivations with the tasks at hand, then the workforce will be engaged.

We are proponents of the book entitled *Intrinsic Motivation at Work: What Really Drives Employee Engagement* by Kenneth W. Thomas. In his book, Thomas describes the need for human beings to find purpose in their work, which requires purposeful leadership—leaders who understand this and work to provide that purpose beyond the need to feed families and have health benefits.

The goal, according to Thomas, is to develop employees that can self-manage, since most work today requires specialized skills that most leaders don't have. Consequently, they must rely on those with the know-how to get the job done without intense oversight and management. For Thomas, self-management consists of five steps (2009, p. 30):

- Employees commit to a meaningful purpose.
- They choose activities to accomplish the purpose.
- Employees perform those activities.
- They monitor progress toward the

purpose.

- Employees move on if the progress is present, or they go back to steps one or two to start over if the progress is not there.

Thomas goes on to highlight four intrinsic rewards that must be present for the employees to be engaged (2009, p. 50):

- Meaningfulness—employees must have an idea of how their work fits into the meaning of the company's vision and mission.
- Choice—workers must have a say in how their work will be done, especially if they have the expertise necessary to do the job.
- Competency—employees must have a chance to improve their skills and grow professionally.
- Progress—workers must be able to see that their work progress toward the desired outcome with reasonable speed.

It is interesting that we still managed to give AWSS a "Fair" rating in this category, even though AWSS falls woefully short of providing these four intrinsic motivators. Morale is low due to poor communication and lack of vision (or at least not a vision that is shared by everyone). Leadership, specifically CEO Ben Holiday, is not in touch with what is most important to his employees, having made the assumption that money is the only motivator to get people to do their jobs. When AWSS moved into New York City, their employees lost any sense of connection with their local community, and found themselves among the nameless, anonymous thousands making the long trek into the City every day.

Even though we found all that to be true, the people still "soldiered" on and found intrinsic motivation in the long-term clients they served, taking emotional sustenance from the company's distinguished past. It is surprising to us that, in spite of current conditions, there is still a sense of family among those remaining with the company. That is a testament not to good leadership. Rather it is a reflection to the commitment many employees have in the modern workforce to do their best not *because of* their company's leadership but *in spite of* it.

We found there to be little sense of teamwork, or as we like to refer to it as inclusion, since most people do not feel involved in the decision-making process at AWSS. Their sense of being excluded from the vision of the company is exacerbated by the woeful communication system that includes rumors, threats, and half-truths. When leadership does not communicate meaning to their followers, the followers make up their own meaning, and it is usually inaccurate and inflammatory. That is the exact scenario that currently exists at AWSS.

Our team-building sessions and one-on-one interviews with the AWSS staff have uncovered a massive disconnect between leadership and the rest of the team that was highlighted and intensified around the decision to be involved in the domestic surveillance program. Most of the employees did not complain about their pay, but had serious questions about the purpose of the jobs they were asked to perform. Many had no interest in being "spies" carrying out the surveillance initiative, no matter how good the pay was.

We strongly urge AWSS leadership to recognize the disengaged atmosphere that currently exists at the company, and to allow MCC consultants to assist in regaining an atmosphere that is conducive to an engaged workforce.

## Resilience

The letter "R" in the L.E.A.D.E.R.S. Model stands for resilience, which literally means to "bounce back." Resilience is that hard-to-explain human characteristic that gives people the ability to withstand and positively respond to the challenges of life. This resilience allows them to rebound from difficult circumstances and emerge ready to move forward with even greater resolve. Historically, resilience is often equated with those who experienced the Great Depression. The so-called "Greatest Generation" endured the tremendous economic and personal challenges present during those years and emerged ready to engage in the next ultimate challenge: World War II.

Today, resilience is considered an important individual as well as organizational trait and is especially relevant given the often chaotic and uncertain landscape in today's corporate world. Resilience is one of the qualities of a "positive" organizational environment in which employees are much better suited to deal with the pace of change they face while continuing to work towards the fulfillment of their company's vision and mission. It is this "bend but not break" attitude and behavior that enables employees to remain positive and productive while under the stress, thus ensuring organizational success.

Various studies have shown that individuals who are resilient are generally positive in their outlook. They believe their life, and life in general, has ultimate worth. Those who are resilient are more likely to accept their life circumstances, and are able to make do in whatever situation they may find themselves—figuratively to "turn lemons into lemonades" (Coutu, 2002).

An encouraging aspect of resilience is that it can be understood and developed regardless of one's background or position within an organization. Those in leadership roles have a unique responsibility to create work environments that support the development and existence of resilience among co-workers. Leaders must model the behaviors of resilience by being positive and optimistic, fostering a climate of mutual support, and seeing failure (in themselves or others) as a learning experience. Leaders who encourage the growth of re-silience make their organizations intrinsically-motivating places to work, especially during times of challenge and change.

There is more emphasis today on cognitive issues and practices when it comes to leadership and resilience. In other words, the practice of resilience starts with how people think. If they believe things will improve, for example, they can control their "self talk," encouraging themselves that better days are ahead. Cognitive theory begins with the belief that one's emotional state comes not from adversity but from one's *belief* about adversity.

For example, the U. S. Army instituted a program to build resilience by looking to develop three key areas in their recruits: mental toughness, signature strengths, and strong relationships. Drill sergeants, in particular, participate in this program first to build their own resil-iency capacity and then to pass it along to those soldiers who are under their command (Seligman, 2011).

Author Rich Fernandez recommends five prac-tices that can increase resilience among individuals in organizations. These include:

- *practicing mindfulness*—being aware of events and experiences as they occur;

- *compartmentalizing work during the day*—focusing on one particular task or assignment at a time, as opposed to multitasking;
- *taking short breaks every hour and a half to two hours*—stepping away from the task at hand to mentally refresh;
- *develop the ability to respond not just react to difficult situations or people*—the ability to pause, step back, reflect, shift perspectives, create options, and choose wisely;
- *cultivate compassion*—both self-compassion and compassion for others (Fernandez, 2016).

Let's look at one more point. Developing the capacity of resilience, both for leaders and their co-workers, is related to the level of Emotional Intelligence (EI) of those individuals. EI has been a popular topic of discussion in leadership circles, so we will not go into much detail here. It is important to understand that emotional intelligence includes the notion of "self-awareness." This trait includes knowing ourselves and managing our emotions; knowing the social needs of others; and managing social relationships by understanding the impact of what we do and say has on those relationships. EI gives us the ability to increase self-esteem, express thoughtful, active concern for others, and demonstrate the flexibility to adapt to changes that may create difficult circumstances. Thus, as individual EI grows, so does resilience.

Ben's top-down leadership style and just-do-it personality have weakened the organization to the point of collapse. To Ben, resilience simply means to "suck it up" so he tells employees to "deal with it" when it comes to facing company's adversity. Ben has no clue that, when he made the unilateral decisions to engage the domestic surveillance initiative, it led to a tremendous loss of company morale. When confronted with this reality, Ben responded to his leadership team's pushback by firing Tommy and several of his co-workers who voiced strong disapproval over the domestic surveillance initiative.

Despite this lack of understanding and resilience-building by Ben, there is a surprising level of individual resilience among a number of AWSS employees. These folks have "stuck with it," even though the work environment Ben has created does not encourage such behaviors. This is no doubt a combination of personal qualities and the artifact of commitment to AWSS that was instilled by the positive leadership of Ben's predecessors.

How can AWSS build the kind of organizational resilience that is necessary for it to again achieve the type of missional and financial success that was the case under Ben's predecessors? It's going to be a great challenge. Since so much of the responsibility of creating the capacity of resilience among employees typically falls on the leaders, AWSS will struggle to make any progress in this area. Ben does not reflect the qualities of a leader who is resilient and who can encourage and develop resilience in others at AWSS. As stated previously in this section, leaders who are positive and optimistic, and who are supportive and reassuring, use these practices and behaviors to build resilience among those they lead.

Consequently, for AWSS to be more resilient, Ben needs to change, which is a common theme throughout this report. Ben must realize the importance of having a resilient organization and understand that for this to exist, resilience must begin with him. He needs to consider all of the previous discussion regarding the L.E.A.D.E.R.S. Model and how his shortcomings in these areas impact his ability to develop resilience in himself and for AWSS. Since resilience is the sixth practice in the Model, we would recommend that Ben heed the recommendations in the previous five steps. As he does that, employees will hopefully respond to his efforts and the changes they see, and the organization will hopefully find new reservoirs of resilience that will help AWSS survive and thrive.

While MCC is ready to work with AWSS as a whole, there is a great need for Ben Holiday to engage the services of a personal coach or mentor, someone who can help develop the personal skills and characteristics needed for modern leadership challenges. We suspect that perhaps Mr. Holiday has never addressed the need for people skills, something he would refer to as a "soft skill," and his lack of these behaviors shows up in the company's performance. We stand ready to assist Mr. Holiday in this important work of professional development.

## Stewardship

The letter S in the LEADERS acronym represents the concept of stewardship. Stewardship is an archaic word that was used to describe a person who served in some support capacity, such as a butler or maid. Today the word is still used in some circles, like the cabin steward on a cruise line, the wine steward in a restaurant, or a stewardship campaign in a nonprofit institution that raises money. Those two remaining modern usages—service and money—are the reasons why we have included stewardship as the final trait of effective L.E.A.D.E.R.S.

Each generation of leadership in an organization receives a tremendous trust that they are expected to steward, maintain, and pass on with improvements that will enable future generations to continue to find success. In a sense, leaders first steward the vision and mission of the organization. Then they steward the financial and physical resources they inherit. Then they exercise stewardship over the human resources, the lives of those who contract to work for them. Those workers represent families who have dreams and goals, and who want to steward their own futures for posterity. In other words, stewardship for leaders begins with what they have at present.

Leaders who understand the concept of stewardship desire to leave the world a better place than when they entered it. They realize that their opportunity to make an impact should leave those with whom they do business better people than before they met, and that includes customers, clients, employees, suppliers, and competitors. Leaders understand that the vison of their company is also something that has been loaned to them so they can steward its possibilities, growing the institution. At the same time, leaders see their human resources as a chance to be good stewards as they seek to partner to help those human resources realize their potential.

In the United States, corporations, both for-profit and nonprofit, are treated in some respects as individuals. Those organizations have rights and responsibilities; they can sue and be sued; and they pay taxes and receive tax breaks for certain activities that the Federal Government deems are in the public interest. Therefore, it is not unusual to consider corporate social responsibilities just like we would consider responsibilities for individual citizens.

First, let's look at the fiscal responsibilities that organizations have. If they are publicly-held corporations, those responsibilities are to their shareholders to conduct business in a manner where a profit is realized, and dividends are distributed to the investors. If the company is not publicly traded, the company still has a responsibility to its workers to share the profits their work has generated with them.

Then there should be a sense among institutions that they do not exist in a vacuum. They have neighbors and a local community in which their business functions. As an individual would be expected to be a good neighbor, organizations are expected to do the same. This is not only an obligation in the mind of some, it makes good business sense to others. A healthy community contributes to the health of that organization's local operation, and the wise company invests in the health of the community as a means of enhancing its own health.

Years ago, someone coined the term "triple bottom line" that included three areas that all business entities need to manage. That triple bottom line is people, planet, and profit, in that order. We found evidence that in its history, AWSS followed this general rule well before it was ever defined.

The vision of the AWSS founders was to provide quality security through quality people. Their purpose as expressed as follows:

> AWSS exists to provide companies and institutions with peace of mind that their property and business interests are secure while providing a world-class place of employment for all employees.

The founders invested in the community by building a park and establishing a library for the local residents. This garnered much goodwill from the local community, providing an open door to local officials and winning the goodwill of neighbors, who tolerated the occasional traffic or other inconvenience that the AWSS headquarters created. It is of note that AWSS was among the first to produce what is now known as a "green" building, something one would not expect from a security company.

The founders also invested in their employees, saying thank you for their contributions to the company's success. There were rewards and special recognitions. The company assisted children of employees with their college expenses, and provided tuition reimbursement for employees who went back to school in the area of expertise for which the company had hired them. If employees did not go back to school, there was a generous budget for training workshops and seminars that would contribute to the personal and professional growth of the employees.

All that came to a halt under Ben's leadership. Even before the business downturn, training and travel budgets were slashed or eliminated, and the tuition reimbursement and scholarship program were abandoned. Long-term employees, once the darling of the organization for their commitment and wisdom, were gradually laid off with little attention paid to their past performance and sacrifice on behalf of the company. Several people mentioned in their interviews how angry they were over how one man, Charlie Mitchell, had been treated. Mr. Mitchell was let go 18 months short of his retirement, after investing 32 years with AWSS. There was a small office party, but nothing else was done to honor his outstanding contributions.

Financial management is the first area of stewardship that is part of effective leadership. The second area of stewardship is service. Leaders must become stewards of the company vision, ensuring that it is fulfilled in a way that maximizes the benefits for the various stakeholders of the company—staff, vendors, clients or customers, the community, and the world at large.

Any institution that consumes resources to produce a product or service, and those resources may be physical, financial or human, has a responsibility to use those resources in a manner that helps or at least does not harm the best interests of those stakeholders.

AWSS has created a serious issue for itself concerning the domestic surveillance program that Ben insisted on and surreptitiously launched. When the media furor hit over the controversial nature of the practice, the company's future was put at risk. The controversy not only caused AWSS' reputation to suffer, but it cost the company some of its most talented managers and leaders. A case can be made that Ben made a decision that was inconsistent with the founder's vision of quality security through quality people. We consider this a break of the stewardship responsibility incumbent upon the company's leadership. From our interviews with staff, it is clear that Ben was the main instigator and proponent of this program, exhibiting once again a poor sense of stewardship for the company's vision and values.

What's more, Ben has not recognized his responsibility to steward its human resources in a manner that is ethical and consistent with company values. People like Charlie Mitchell had been their greatest asset, but Ben ignored any obligation he had to honor his services (and others like him) so were also guilty of poor stewardship where human lives were concerned.

Like in many other areas of the L.E.A.D.E.R.S. Model, we assigned AWSS a "poor" rating in the area of stewardship. While we assign this to the company, it is really an indictment against the entire leadership team, of which we could only find one member—Ben Holiday. We will outline in another document the services we can provide to assist AWSS and Ben improve in this important area. It is obvious that outside help is needed if the company is to face the realities of where it is and where it will be if immediate action isn't taken.

In addition to team-building efforts, we highly recommend that the company go through a rigorous process to reconnect with its corporate values, which have largely been ignored, and especially to re-focus on its purpose or mission statement. If the current statement is no longer relevant, a new one can be developed. This statement cannot be mere words on a piece of paper, however, but must represent something the company sees as almost sacred and worthy of their energies. In other words, they must become stewards of the vision, serving it and not expecting it to serve them.

That completes my evaluation of the current situation at AWSS. I present these findings in the interest of creating a dialogue about the way forward in order that AWSS may recapture its vitality and vigor as a leading force in the security industry. Never before have there been greater threats to freedom and a greater need for reliable security services, even at the residential level. I look forward to working with Mr. Holiday and the AWSS team to help turn things around to recapture the glory and success that were once theirs.

Respectfully submitted,

Francis Johnson

# Interview
# with the Authors

# An Interview with the Authors of *A Leadership Carol*

## Jim Dittmar and John W. Stanko

**JD:** For 20 years, I was the director of the Geneva College Masters in Science Organizational Leadership Program (MSOL) and chair of the Department of Leadership Studies. Over the years, we had created a large repository of information about leadership, not just theories but practical applications. It was so rewarding to hear people express, at the end of this two-year graduate program for working adults and professionals, how the program had transformed their lives, not just at work but holistically. Our graduates did not approach leadership as they had before they started.

**JS:** And I will forever be grateful that I got involved. There were so many aspects of the program that were special. As I taught leadership through both the faith-based and humanistic principles in each course, it made me a better leader, author, and teacher. It made me better at everything I do because it was comprehensive, relevant, and practical. I saw the transformation that took place in each student's life, some of whom wept openly during their final presentations because of the power in the material, not just to stimulate their mind, but to impact their hearts.

**JD:** You mentioned the integration of faith perspectives in the classroom, done in a way that was comprehensive but not overwhelming. The course material, however, was also integrated in another way. We offered ten courses during the two-year program and we integrated concepts across courses, so it was also interdisciplinary. There were ideas we talked about in one particular course that we would carry into the next course, or a course offered a year later. Our belief was leadership involved a variety of skills, traits, behaviors, and disciplines.

Therefore, we taught communication, ethics, professional development, motivation, decision making, change, research, finance, and strategy—all from a leadership perspective. You may be engaged in any of those activities or rely on concepts from those areas when you are serving as a leader. Our faculty needed to be aware not just of their own course or expertise; they had to have an understanding of the entire program curriculum and how their particular course or emphasis impacted the other classes and leadership skills being taught. There was a commitment beyond just coming in to teach a course, so we had part-time and full-time faculty making a difference as together they fulfilled the vision and mission of the MSOL program.

**JS:** An aspect of the program that was so vital and important was each student developing his or definition of leadership. We would watch their definition morph from what they wrote in their very first class. Then as part of their final presentation, they would spell out their new definition and explain all the important words and phrases included in that definition. I had never even done that as a leader and teacher of leadership principles. If I was going to be a part of the MSOL program, I had to come up with my own definition of leadership. I say that because it was important for us as we worked on this book together to draw from what we had taught and learned to put something forth that would contribute to the understanding of leadership for our readers. That's where the L.E.A.D.E.R.S. Model came from, for it emanates from the various aspects of leadership that we learned in the MSOL program.

JD: Again, that's another distinctive of the MSOL program. We sought a way for students to have some capstone experience where they could make sense of all the things we had talked about over the course of the program. They had to make choices and determine what were the critical key ideas that are part of leadership from their perspective. I told my students to look at their final project this way: If you were walking down the main street of the area you live and someone stopped you and asked, "What is leadership?", what would you tell them? Furthermore, if that person asked where you got that from, what would you tell them? Those same questions led us to write this book. We wanted to draw from that reservoir of all the leadership knowledge we have in creating this story we call *A Leadership Carol*. While we told the story, we wanted to develop our own leadership model that captured what we had been teaching and talking about over the years and apply those concepts to the characters in the story.

JS: We also emphasized to the students that this was only the beginning of their leadership journey. The MSOL program was sensitizing them to the need for regular leadership challenges and inputs into their lives that would cause them to grow and learn. During the program, they were exposed to authors they enjoyed and who impacted their lives. From then on, if they would see an article or a new book, they would want to stay in touch with what that author's current thinking was concerning leadership. We wanted them to pursue the extraordinary and to continue the work of developing their leadership philosophy, values, and expressions. So for us, we wanted to write something that would continue to add to their understanding, and to ours. We had challenged them to continue to grow, but now we had to continue to grow, develop, produce, contribute, and learn. This book project certainly did that for me.

Earlier last year, Jim and I met at a place where we used to teach and sat in a classroom, just to talk. We knew we wanted to write something, but we didn't know how exactly to proceed. It was just after the Christmas season, and somehow the concept emerged and we started to talk about the classic movie *A Christmas Carol*. Dickens' original work actually had a sociological message because the poor were being marginalized in his day, and he was making a statement to hold them in our hearts all year round.

We started talking about how there were leadership overtones in the movie, and started to sketch out on a board what those leadership principles were. We met two or three more times and worked diligently on it. We were deeply influenced by Ken Blanchard, Pat Lencioni, and others who had written fables and stories as a vehicle to deliver their message and teaching on leadership. We thought we would do the same thing, and thought that *A Christmas Carol* could be the vehicle to do this. We met on Friday mornings for about nine months, and I will never forget the enthusiasm and excitement we had, because we knew we were on to something.

**JD:** We saw how this could work. I think at one point I used the description "a light-hearted adaptation of Dickens' novel, *A Christmas Carol* that teaches timeless or important leadership lessons for today." That was the fun part, because what we had to do is envision how that fit in today's context. In other words, we were creating a modern-day application for some of Dickens' concepts in the original novel. We came up with the idea for this company, and once we had that and had a Scrooge-like character, things began to flow.

JS: The idea of the company emerged out of our discussions. We were feeding off one another's creativity, but we wanted and needed a character like Scrooge. That's where the name Ben came from, E-**Ben**-eezer. We originally planned to have him be a descendent of Ebenezer Scrooge, but that didn't quite make its way into the story. Then we tried to come up with a company concept that we could use to modernize the story that would add some controversy. That's when we came up with security and surveillance. Those hadn't been in the news recently, but still ones that would be open for debate among citizens when they find that someone is spying and gathering information on them.

Since consultants play a role for many companies in their leadership development, we decided to replace the ghost of Christmas past, present, and future, with consultants who would address leadership past, present, and future. Also, we wanted to show that the spirit of the company's founders as expressed in the company's vision and values had guided it well over the years. When Ben violated that vision, even then the spirit of the founders worked to call him back to the foundation that had been laid.

JD: We did not want the story to overwhelm or overshadow the leadership principles. That was the fun part, to determine what we could do in terms of not making the story too complex, but making it understandable and supportive of the leadership principles. This company was founded by people who were good leaders in many respects, and particularly in how they treated people, both internally and externally. Then when Ben's father dies prematurely, Ben takes over and discounts the past and creates his own little world of nastiness through his poor leadership. That causes the company to take a dive, and we wanted to make the connection between good leadership and company performance.

JS: It's interesting that while this is a fictional story, we both have had real-life experiences that helped contribute to this. The scene where Ben relieves Francis of his duties actually happened to me out in California. I was brought in to help build the team, but after a day and a half, the CEO brought me in and said that I wasn't helping. He knew he had lazy people and he needed me to light a fire under them, so he handed me my check and sent me on my way. As I was leaving, some of the staff asked if I had forgotten something in my car. I informed them I had been relieved of my duties, and they almost wrapped their arms around my legs as I walked to my car, saying, "Please don't go! You've been speaking truth and we need to confront these issues!"

Of course, I love New York, having gone to prep school in Connecticut and often visiting my favorite aunt who lived in New Jersey. Englewood is probably more upscale than what we make it to be in the story, but it is right across the George Washington Bridge. We wanted to make the company family-run, so the characters would have extra incentive to be passionate about the direction AWSS had taken. There's always tremendous loss when we don't treat people the way they should be treated. It's not just altruism, it's good business.

JD: The research is so overwhelmingly clear that good leadership leads to greater production, a healthier workplace, and a host of other positive outcomes. Of course, we know that so often the approach is to cut, cut, cut, and cut some more, rather than increase care and improve performance.

JS: It's a competitive advantage to treat people

in a way that stimulates their creativity and leads them to freely present their gifts, enthusiasm, talents, and experiences for the good of the organization, because it is also for their good.

JD: The consultant angle was a useful one for us, for it allowed our character Francis to generate a report after a week or two with the AWSS team. We alluded to the report throughout the story, but then included it as an addendum to the story that allowed us to present our concept of the L.E.A.D.E.R.S. Model while showing how that model could and should play out in real life. While we are telling the story, we are using the report to explain the L.E.A.D.E.R.S. Model. The consultants who visit Ben's home also reference the report to explain the critical issues that are destroying the company, debilitating the people, and having a negative impact on the community where they originally had the business. The story is not too complex that you need a scorecard to keep track of who's who, but provides enough substance through which we could present the significant fundamental leadership principles we believe to be essential for any effective leader.

JS: We wanted Ben to feel some sense of violation just as he had violated other people, so the consultants came to his home and used his TV to record the sessions. Of course, the final consultant is a shock to him because even though she is from the future, she's really a voice from the past who is a family member calling him to account. We had a lot of fun with the story, but we really were quite serious with the consultant's report. The story was the fictional vehicle to bring our non-fictional L.E.A.D.E.R.S. Model to life. I did perhaps a little more work with the story, but Dr. Jim did a lot more work with the L.E.A.D.E.R.S. Model.

JD: As I said earlier, we tried to pull on the

reservoir of knowledge over these last twenty years as we developed our Model, and that's where the L.E.A.D.E.R.S. Model came from. The first letter L stands for leadership. We believe leadership is fundamentally relational. That's where it starts, and that has huge implications as we explain in our consultant's report. Then E stands for ethics. We know there are some authors who equate good leadership with ethical leadership. Without an ethical framework and commitment to establish and maintain ethical standards and behaviors, there are eventually going to be problems in any organization.

**JS:** Since we were drawing material from a faith-integrated program, it wasn't a big leap for us to make ethics the second component. It really is, or should be, a foundational piece. You can do a lot of good things in an organization, but if you do illegal or unethical things, the whole institution can collapse like a house of cards.

**JD:** One of the things we emphasize in the ethics discussion is that how leaders treat people is just as important as the leader's financial and fiduciary responsibilities. If the leader is unethical in the way he or she leads people, the way they treat others, the way they structure people's jobs, and the way people are rewarded, it goes back to what we mentioned under the letter L for leadership. It's a relational issue, and that can have ethical ramifications. We try to show that this is where Ben was off the mark—in the way he treated people—and we see that kind of behavior as an ethical violation.

**JS:** I've done a lot of work, and Dr. Jim you have too, with non profits and churches. We have found that those organizations will be diligent not to waste ten cents, but they waste their human resources regularly. We make a statement that this is an ethical issue, not just an efficiency issue.

**JD:** Moving on to the letter A, which stands for

the concept of alignment. Alignment is also important, for people must understand the meaning, value, and purpose of their work. They are aligned when they know how what they are doing is contributing directly to the fulfillment of that vision, mission, and goals of the organization. If I understand how my work is aligned with and helping to fulfill the vision, and mission today, next week, and three months from now, then that contributes positively to organizational performance and achievement. We see it as the leadership's responsibility to ensure that everything necessary to create that alignment is in place. Alignment has also been called line-of-sight, for it allows anyone to see from where they are to the CEO's office, or anywhere else in the organization.

Alignment is what it takes for a leader to create a strong commitment within the organization among people. After the A for alignment, D is for decision making. If leaders do nothing else all day, they make decisions, as do others throughout the organization. As fundamental of a practice as decision making is, there are things about it that are often ignored. Therefore, we try to show how leaders can become better at making quality decisions. After the D, E is for engagement. Engagement relates to motivation, and is a practice to ensure that people are giving all they have to give, and not holding back energy, creativity, or teamwork. Then we move on to R, which stands for resilience, which is a concept we don't hear a lot about necessarily. It's the idea that people can go through difficult and challenging times, and not only endure, not only continue to function, but they come out on the other side in better shape than before. And so that's important. How does a leader create an organization environment in which resilience is a quality of the people?

**JS:** No matter how good a leader you are, there

may be situations in the economy or in world affairs that could negatively impact your business. We saw that after 9/11, and we've seen that in other situations where there were unethical banking practices that caused many people to suffer, along with the entire economy. Resiliency is vital, not only because we are imperfect humans and our leadership may be flawed, but life is uncertain and stuff happens. Leaders have to be prepared to respond to those things beyond their control, by keeping control of the things they can control. That's why we wanted to include resilience in the L.E.A.D.E.R.S. Model.

JD: And then finally, the S is for stewardship. That has gotten a little more press these days than it would have 15 or 20 years ago. To what does the concept of stewardship or being a steward refer? It's not just financial stewardship, but it's stewardship of people, of the organization's mission, of the environment, and of the community where the organization resides. Some people use the phrase "triple bottom line" that refers to people, planet, and profit, in that order of importance. And again, if we reorder our understanding in terms of what it means to be a true steward, it means that the organization is on loan to the leaders. It's given to them to steward and to make it better by the time they leave than when they got there.

JS: We didn't want this model to be complex, and it shouldn't be, for often good leadership is intuition combined with a bit of common sense. It is treating people the way we would want to be treated. This fictitious company called AWSS needed a good dose of what we called SIC principles in all areas of leadership.

The acronym SIC stands first for service, and then the I is for Inclusion, which is another word for team building. It's bringing as many people to the table as possible, at any level of the organization. Dr. Jim, you championed the decision making chapter and inclusion is very important for you. You repeat over and over again to make sure you have the right people at the table when you're about to make a decision. That's inclusion. Also, engagement is inclusion. Ethics involves inclusion, for leaders assume they have the only right perspective. Suddenly when they include other people's perspectives, they realize it's not as simple an ethical decision or process as they had first imagined. There still may be one ethical answer. It may become clear, but as it's discussed, there are various perspectives, and listening to those will allow the leaders to know where people need to be persuaded and influenced, and where sometimes the leader must be influenced by the people who are being included in the discussions.

JD: Inclusion is a mindset. If you are exclusive as a leader and you're holed up in a corner and you think you've got it all, one author describes that as functional atheism. That leader doesn't need to believe in anyone else but himself (or herself). They have all the answers and perspectives. This is what Ben did and how he behaved.

JS: The final letter in SIC is the C, and that stands for communication. That was our second class in the order of classes in the MSOL program. It was put second for a reason, for it is certainly foundational. I can't think of a class in which we didn't refer back to communication. I'm of the philosophy in my own consulting business and leadership opportunities that I can't communicate too much. It has to be done in various ways, not just face to face.

Sometimes it's one-on-one, sometimes it's groups, sometimes it's via social media, sometimes it's question and answers, sometimes it's video or a blog or website. We are advocates for communicating, and doing a lot of it. Whether you're involved in leadership itself, ethics, alignment, decision making, engagement, resilience or stewardship—all of those are undergirded by the SIC principles: service, inclusion, and communication. So, we refer to those and kind of call them the seasoning for our leadership stew. The L.E.A.D.E.R.S. Model was the main dish, but we heavily seasoned the dish with our three SIC spices.

JD: Perhaps we should say those three concepts are the vitamins for organizational SIC-ness. There has to be a servant's perspective. The leader has to think, "I'm here to serve. It's not about me, it's about you" for the L.E.A.D.E.R.S. Model to work. There has to be a perspective of inclusion that invigorates and influences the actions and activities that leaders take. And where communication is concerned, leadership is not going to be relational if there isn't a lot of communication. You're not going to have alignment or make effective decisions if there isn't communication. As John said, there's no such thing as over-communicating. Talk to anyone in an organization and ask what one of their issues is that's going on. . .

JS: And they say, "We don't know what's going on around here and that no one talks to us." Leadership, along with whoever they have included in their discussions, will wrestle with issues and decisions for hours, weeks, maybe even months. They come to a conclusion, and present it as final. It's baked and already done, and they expect everyone to be on the same page in a short amount of time, when it took them a long time to get on the same page themselves. Therefore, we appeal to leaders to give their followers, those not involved in the decision-making process, as much time as they had (if possible) to come to the conclusion they did.

So Jim, which concept stands out to you as the primary and most important one?

JD: I think the L for leadership is right where it needs to be at the beginning because it defines the framework for every other component. Our first course in the MSOL program was the History and Theory of Leadership, and it was in that place for a reason. That course lays a foundation of not only leadership concepts, but also other very important models and concepts related to leadership. If you don't understand that leadership is fundamentally relational, that it's not about the leader and not about the position, but rather about the process of engaging others around some change, movement, or objective, then leadership is always going to be less than it could be. In that first course, we introduce students to an author, Joseph Rost, who wrote a book in the early 90's titled *Leadership for the 21st Century*. Rost is really the one who first talked in-depth about defining leadership as an influence relationship, a process of influencing people through relationships towards the accomplishment of a mutual goal, purpose, intent, or change.

JS: The first class I ever taught in the MSOL Program was motivation, so the E for engagement for me is the key. Engaging people by building on their strengths means that I as the leader know what strengths they have, or even before that, help them know what strengths they have. I as the leader want people to be able and free to communicate what those strengths are, and then to serve those people to create opportunities where they have, on a regular basis, an opportunity to do what it is they love to do—what it is that they do best. When that occurs, they feel engaged in what they are doing.

We learn through one of our courses in the MSOL program that an engaged workforce is self-managing.

They make the choices and decisions of how their work is going to be done, instead of being micromanaged and having it imposed on them. We understand there are exceptions to the engagement, so sometimes workers have to be brought along to the point where they are able to do just that.

In the book, we show that while Ben thought he had the best ideas for the organization, those ideas and the sense of the history for the organization resided more completely in guys like Tommy, Jimmy, and others who were at odds with Ben because he was trying to say, "I will tell you what to do, and you just do it. If I want your opinion, I'll give it to you." They were not being adversarial, but whenever the leadership position is controlling rather than relational, then anyone who tries to question or take a position that is contrary to what the leader wants, is considered to be adversarial or combative. When that happens, people shut down. When people shut down, we lose the best of who they are, and that includes their creativity, energy, enthusiasm, passion, ideas, and hard work. They start to give their minimum, and when that happens, everyone loses.

**JS:** If you have gotten this far, we trust you have read this book. As we conclude, we hope, as we said earlier, that this will contribute in two ways to your own leadership journey. One, it will give you some additional insight, maybe a review of what you have known. You could be busy and aren't keeping up and aren't taking stock and inventory of your own leadership style or philosophy. Maybe you're taking shortcuts. We hope this will help you understand that leadership is something you need to be working on all the time.

There is never a down time. As soon as you relax, you start to rely on what you have done in the past. You start to rely on your title and you resort to telling people what to do as opposed to influencing or persuading them as you build a relationship with them that will engage them and cause them to give their best. We hope that you read through the consultant's report and ask where you are in all of that as you read, asking yourself, "Where does my company show up in this? Where does my leadership show up in this? And in the L.E.A.D.E.R.S. Model? Where is my organization sick in the wrong way, instead of involving SIC in the right way?" We hope you will be challenged in what you are doing, and we further hope that this will create a hunger in people.

JD: For some, it may be more of a challenge than a revisit or a reminder. We hope some leaders confront Ben and see him as a reflection of their own image. It's difficult to change leadership behavior. It doesn't happen overnight. Ben begins to change his perspectives and attitudes rather quickly but it still takes a while for him to really change how he acts as a leader. Scrooge began to behave differently the very next morning. Few change that dramatically in one evening or one night as Scrooge did. We understand that this process of becoming the leader and engaging in leadership in the way we describe it takes time. It requires reflection and change.

One of the strengths of the MSOL program is that we created an environment where people could be intentionally reflective. They could challenge their own assumptions and what they thought they believed. It was through that process of challenging assumptions and the ability to reflect on them when we saw students admit they did not think like that any longer. That was our goal: That the students would be transformed because they thought differently than before they entered the program. Their thoughts allowed them to act differently, and they were transformed. Then once they were transformed, they could lead a transformation in their group, department, organization, or at whatever level they were at. We hope that's what happens as a result of someone reading this book.

**JS:** This was your first venture into book writing. Do you think it will be your last?

**JD:** No. It was important for me to have a collaborator since I have not done this before, and it was that collaborative process that made it work for me. In many ways, I am a collaborator. I enjoy working together with others. I enjoy the creative synergy that comes as a result of that. I think that's what happened here. Therefore, I hope to keep doing some writing in this way, individually and collaboratively.

**JS:** This project was a great experience for me. This was my first collaborative experience after writing many books on my own. I have contributed to other works, but never in a truly collaborative way. In many ways, you and I had to apply what we were writing about as we worked together. We had to be in alignment and make decisions. We were engaged. There were weeks it didn't seem like we were making any progress, so we had to be resilient. We also had to be good stewards. We had an idea for this project, not only for this creative project, but ideas about leadership, and we wanted to get them out there to the public.

# Jim Dittmar Bio

For more than 30 years, Jim Dittmar has served in the field of leadership development as a practitioner, teacher, consultant, researcher, and author. He is the founder, president, and CEO of 3Rivers Leadership Institute. Prior to this, Jim was the founder and director of the Geneva College M.S. in Organizational Leadership Program. Through the 3Rivers Leadership Institute, Jim provides training and learning experiences that include a strong grounding not only in the "what" that leaders face but also in the "how" and "so what" in terms of driving these issues to the practical, behavioral level. It is through this process of reflection and application that participants experience leadership development that is truly transformational. This is Jim's first collaborative book project.

# John W. Stanko Bio

John founded a personal and leadership development company, called *PurposeQuest*, in 2001 and today travels the world to speak, consult and inspire leaders and people everywhere. From 2001-2008, he spent six months a year in Africa and still enjoys visiting and working on that continent, while teaching for Geneva College's Master of Science in Leadership Studies and at the Center for Urban Biblical Ministry in his hometown of Pittsburgh, Pennsylvania. Most recently, John founded Urban Press, a publishing service designed to tell stories of the city, from the city and to the city. John is the author of 30 books.

# References

Coutu, Diane L. (2002). How resilience works. *Harvard Business Review*, 80(5), 46-56.

Fernandez, Richard (2016). Five ways to build your personal resilience at work. Retrieved from https://hbr.org/2016/06/627-building-resilience-ic-5-ways-to-build-your-personal-resilience-at-work

Kohn, Alfie. (1999) *Punished by Rewards: The Trouble with Gold Stars, Incentive Plans, A's, Praise, and Other Bribes*. Boston: Houghlin Mifflin Company.

McCall, M.W., Jr. & Kaplan, R.E. (1989). *Whatever it takes: The realities of managerial decision making*, 2nd ed. Pearson.

Rost, Joseph (1993). *Leadership for the 21st Century*. Westport, Conn: Praeger.

Seligman, Martin E. (2011). Building resilience. *Harvard Business Review*, 89(4), 100-106.

Thomas, Kenneth W. (2009). *Intrinsic Motivation at Work: What Really Drives Employee Engagement*. San Francisco: Berret-Kohler Publishers Inc. 51-56

# contact Information

### Jim Dittmar
jimdittmar@jimdittmar.com
www.jimdittmar.com
724.462.9962

### John Stanko
johnstanko@gmail.com
www.johnstanko.us
www.purposequest.com
412.646.2780

Made in the USA
Middletown, DE
21 July 2017